How to Get the Most
Out of Philosophy

How to Get the Most Out of Philosophy

Second Edition

DOUGLAS J. SOCCIO

SHASTA COLLEGE

Wadsworth Publishing Company
Belmont, California
I(T)P   **An International Thomson Publishing Company**

Belmont • Albany • Bonn • Boston • Cincinnati • Detroit • London • Madrid • Melbourne
Mexico City • New York • Paris • San Francisco • Singapore • Tokyo • Toronto • Washington

Philosophy Editor: Tammy Goldfeld
Editorial Assistant: Kelly Zavislak
Production Editor: Carol Carreon Lombardi
Cover and interior design: Andrew H. Ogus
Print Buyer: Diana Spence
Copy Editor: Barbara Kimmel
Compositor: Steven Bolinger
Printer: Malloy Lithographing, Inc.

Printed in the United States of America
    2 3 4 5 6 7 8 9 10—01 00 99 98 97 96 95
ISBN 0-534-21694-3

For more information, contact Wadsworth Publishing Company:

Wadsworth Publishing Company
10 Davis Drive
Belmont, California 94002, USA

International Thomson Publishing Europe
Berkshire House 168-173
High Holborn
London, WC1V 7AA, England

Thomas Nelson Australia
102 Dodds Street
South Melbourne 3205
Victoria, Australia

Nelson Canada
1120 Birchmount Road
Scarborough, Ontario
Canada M1K 5G4

International Thomson Editores
Campos Eliseos 385, Piso 7
Col. Polanco
11560 México D.F. México

International Thomson Publishing GmbH
Königswinterer Strasse 418
53227 Bonn, Germany

International Thomson Publishing Asia
221 Henderson Road
#05-10 Henderson Building
Singapore 0315

International Thomson Publishing Japan
Hirakawacho Kyowa Building, 3F
2-2-1 Hirakawacho
Chiyoda-ku, Tokyo 102, Japan

For students everywhere—
but especially for first-generation students
and their families

The sages said, "Much wisdom I learned from my teachers, more from colleagues, from my pupils most of all." Even as a small piece of wood kindles a large log, so a pupil of small attainment sharpens the mind of his teacher, so that by his questions, he elicits glorious wisdom.

Maimonides

Contents

Preface to Instructors
(and Curious Students)

I am regularly amazed at the seemingly "obvious" things many of my students don't know at all, or fail to recognize the importance of. Things like reading the course syllabus—and keeping it for the entire term. Things like carefully following formatting instructions for writing assignments. Things like bringing the textbook to class. Things like using the glossary and index. Things like coming by during scheduled office hours and asking questions.

When the first edition of *How to Get the Most Out of Philosophy* came out bundled with *Archetypes of Wisdom*, it generated two kinds of responses. I was both surprised and gratified by the intensity of positive interest. Instructors and students requested additional, stand-alone copies, which, alas, were not available. This expanded second edition is the result of those requests and many helpful suggestions.

A different kind of response to the first edition was more troubling to me. A number of philosophy instructors (not students) trivialized the book as "hokey," "simplistic," and "belaboring the obvious." Perhaps that this second reaction came from instructors whose undergraduate students arrive having completed four years of sophisticated college prep courses in high school. Perhaps many of the more disdainful instructors were themselves good students from highly stable backgrounds and so remain unaware of the kinds of things many promising students simply haven't learned in high school.

For the most part, however, an increasingly diverse student body includes growing numbers of students who are the first members of their families to attend college, as well as many students trying to juggle family responsibilities, jobs, and solid course loads; students from shaky environments; and students who did well enough in high school but still arrive in college a bit naive, disorganized, and perhaps even a little insecure. This book is for those students—and for their instructors.

I know first-hand the consequences of "not knowing the ropes," for I am a first-generation student. I began my college education by driving across town to a pretty good community college. When I was ready to transfer to the local state university for upper division courses, I approached a couple of my favorite instructors for letters of recommendation. I thought that since I had good grades, my instructors would be happy to recommend me to the four-year college. I was wrong—at least initially. They politely informed me that they knew nothing about me. I had never been by their offices, and I had only taken one course from each of them. Eventually, they took pity on me, and after checking my transcript and chatting a while about my plans, they wrote me generic letters.

In hindsight, I understand that as a young man I brought a certain working-class ethic with me to college. One tenet of that ethic is that a person does not use flattery to get ahead. You stand or fall on the quality of your performance, your work. I mistakenly viewed asking my teachers for help outside of class, or just talking with them about their classes, as flattery. Consequently, I deliberately avoided going by to see my instructors. I was so worried about being perceived as a flatterer rather than a hard worker that I deliberately avoided my teachers out of class.

Although I had plenty of love and support from my family, I had no one to teach me about things like letters of recommendation or how to relate to a full-fledged professor. None of us knew much about college—to say nothing of philosophy courses.

My point here is not to tell stories about myself but to point out how easy it is to lose sight of the complexity of factors that bear on student success or failure. The philosophy instructors who reacted so negatively to the first edition may have devoted so much of their attention to the subject matter at hand that they overlooked some of these complicating factors. Today, the great variety of students coming to us to learn philosophy will only increase the usefulness of this book.

We cannot assume that all our students will have graduated from high school with solid writing and thinking skills. In some parts of the country, it is possible to graduate from high school without ever writing an argument paper or analytic essay. Anecdotal literature is quite popular right now, and one consequence is that many students have been required to write only journals and expressive essays and to read expressive—not argumentative—literature. The philosophy course may be the first sustained exposure to critical literature some students have.

How to Get the Most Out of Philosophy, Second Edition, is not intended to compensate for truly remedial skills, nor can its basic advice overcome a truly unstable life circumstance. But it can be just enough of a boost to make a difference between success or failure. Sometimes the smallest help can make a difference.

No matter what kind of philosophy course you teach, no matter where you teach, you are likely to have some students who will benefit from the kind of advice and encouragement it is easy to forget to give—because it seems so obvious to those of us who have been in school nearly all of our lives. It does us wizened old profs—and our students—good to remember that 'twas not always so.

New to the Second Edition

Users of the first edition of *How to Get the Most Out of Philosophy* will note that the second edition has been expanded and reorganized. Changes include:

* The material dealing directly with philosophy has been separated from more general information and moved forward, better reflecting the promise of the title.

- The chapters on critical thinking, critical writing, and critical reading have been expanded and recast.

- Four examples of student writing have been added to Chapter 5, "Critical Writing," so that students can apply their critical skills to writings of varying quality.

- A section on the characteristics of weak, good, and excellent essays has been added to Chapter 5.

- A handy one-page checklist for better critical writing has also been added to Chapter 5.

- A chart for preparing a "time budget" has been added to Chapter 6, "Basic Motivation and Strategy for Getting the Most Out of College"

- Also new to Chapter 6 is an encouraging note to part-time students, who now constitute nearly half of all college students; new material on the biggest mistakes college students make; and a section about the dangers of being too "cool" about school.

- Chapter 7, "Relating to Your Professor" has been updated, and the discussion of letters of recommendation has been enriched.

- This edition contains a new "Beginning Philosopher's Bibliography," with examples of philosophy reference books, general and specialized study skills books, and six writing style guides.

*How to Get the Most
Out of Philosophy*

INTRODUCTION

What To Expect

Have you ever pondered the "big questions"? What's the meaning of life? Is there really a God? If God exists, why does the world seem so crazy? What's wrong with just living for myself? Is everything just a matter of opinion? What is justice? Is everything just a big illusion, some kind of dream?

If you're like almost everybody, you have what I think of as a *philosophical impulse*, a natural curiosity about fundamental questions. Most people seem to respond to this philosophical impulse without prompting. High school and college students sometimes refer to informal philosophical pondering as "bull sessions," and sometimes they are—but not always. Something else may also be going on, something triggered by what Plato and Aristotle (two philosophical megastars) called the *sense of wonder*.

You're possibly wondering what your philosophy course will be like. It won't be another "bull session." Philosophy courses are related to the philosophical impulse in much the same way that joining the school soccer team is related to playing soccer at a picnic with your friends. It's the same game, but the commitment to conditioning and fundamentals and to a schedule set by someone else—and the need to accept the evaluations of an impartial, specially trained referee—can make it seem they are really two completely different games.

Succeeding in a philosophy class requires a willingness to think in a structured, critical way at scheduled times, whether or not you are in a pondering mood—just as being a member of the soccer team requires you to practice or play at scheduled times, whether or not you are in the mood. Your coach may put you in as the goalie when you prefer to play forward—just as your philosophy instructor may want you to think and write about the existence of God when you would rather think and write about the pursuit of pleasure. One of the great sources of student misinformation concerns the overlooked ability to think carefully when not in the mood—just as you have the ability to run wind sprints when you're not in the mood.

So, the first lesson about philosophy courses is that they concern things you are already interested in, but sometimes in a form you may be uncomfortable with at first. One key to success in philosophy class is to begin the term with a firm resolve to participate, whether or not you are in the mood. You have the ability to direct your mind just as you have the ability to pump those exhausted legs for the umpteenth wind sprint. Most of the frustrations students have with philosophy courses can be overcome, or at least reduced to mere annoyances.

This handbook will help you make the most of your philosophy course (and your other courses, as well) by providing useful information and tips about the basic elements that affect your experience in any college course: the subject, the text, the instructor, and your own resolve and circumstances. Although you cannot do anything *directly* about the subject itself or which text your instructor assigns, you can exert considerable influence on yourself and at least some influence on your instructor.

How to Get the Most Out of Philosophy, Second Edition, is based on articles and books about teaching and on conversations with instructors at community colleges, private liberal arts colleges, state universities, and world-famous research universities. Most of all, it is based on my interactions with thousands of students of almost every conceivable background and ability.

Some of the information that follows may be new to you, and some of it will be the same old stuff you've heard most of your life. The point of hearing it again is what the nineteenth-century Danish philosopher Søren Kierkegaard called *edification,* a lesson that *changes us* for the better. Sometimes, we can be encouraged and motivated when someone else says what we already know.

I have made explanations and examples deliberately brief so that you can quickly scan the entire book and then return to pertinent sections as often as you need to. Everything that follows is designed to help you study efficiently, take advantage of the accumulated wisdom of philosophy students and instructors, avoid unnecessary anxiety, get a satisfactory grade, and learn something of value. When the same advice occurs in more than one place, it's there to make it easier for you to review individual sections (say, just the section on essay tests) with assurance that all the basics are there.

You can read *How to Get the Most Out of Philosophy* relatively quickly, and I highly recommend reading it straight through right away. Doing so will get you fired up about philosophy, about your education, and about yourself. Then, you can return to various sections as needed for encouragement, advice, or reminders.

I hope you find philosophy as valuable and interesting as I did when I was a freshman. Please accept this book as part of my way of saying thank you to all my teachers, so many of whom have been my students.

PART ONE

Philosophy Courses

If you've never taken a philosophy course, you're probably curious about what you're getting into. Most college students have had science courses, history classes, literature and English courses, and social science classes in high school. But for most undergraduates, philosophy is new territory.

Chapter 1 discusses special features of philosophy courses and offers suggestions to help you avoid some of the more common anxieties and pitfalls that can slow down beginning philosophy students. Chapter 2 alerts you to important features of philosophical writing.

CHAPTER 1

How To Survive A Philosophy Class

Regardless of the specific format or content of your introductory philosophy courses, you will be encouraged to think for yourself in a critical and sophisticated way, to re-create others' arguments fairly and accurately, and to provide reasons for any position you take on philosophical topics.

Most philosophy courses focus on extended arguments used to justify value judgments and truth claims, the search for very basic principles, standards of meaning and knowledge, and so forth. As a general rule, philosophical questions cannot be settled by the empirical sciences or appeals to religious faith—although scientific evidence and religious beliefs do play a role in some philosophical speculation. Philosophical questions cannot be settled by appeals to personal conviction and experience, or by referring to psychological or social causes—although they, too, play a role in philosophical thinking.

The following passage from René Descartes' (1596–1650) *Rules for the Direction of the Mind* reminds us that our beliefs remain shaky and "second hand," not really ours, until we think them through for ourselves:

> Further, supposing now that all were wholly open and candid, and never thrust upon us doubtful positions as true, but expounded every matter in good faith, yet since scarce anything has been asserted by any one man the contrary of which has not been alleged by another, we should be eternally uncertain which of the two to believe. It would be no use to total up the testimonies in favour of each, meaning to follow that opinion which is supported by the greater number of authors; for if it is a question of difficulty that is in dispute, it is more likely that the truth would have been discovered by few than by many. But even though all these men agreed among themselves, what they teach would not suffice for us. For we shall not, e.g., turn out to be mathematicians though we know by heart all the proofs others have elaborated, unless we have an intellectual talent that fits us to resolve difficulties of any kind. Neither, though we may have mastered all the arguments of Plato and Aristotle, if yet we have not the capacity for passing solid judgment on these matters, shall we become Philosophers; we should have acquired the knowledge not of a [philosophy], but of history.

Philosophy instructors want to help you acquire philosophical understanding, not just information or empty technique. They are as interested in your learning to ask the right questions as they are in helping you get the right answers. You will not be expected to "solve" or "settle" great philosophical issues, only to understand some basic ones, and to think carefully about them.

Because philosophers themselves disagree about the proper way to philosophize, there are no universally accepted formulas to follow in philosophy courses as there are in math or science courses. Your philosophy instructor may disagree with many things in this book, for carefully thought out reasons. If your school has more than one introductory philosophy teacher, you won't be surprised to find that different teachers have different approaches to the "same course." Next time you're in the bookstore, check on the texts used in different sections of the same course. They'll give you some idea of how much variety there can be in one philosophy department.

Most likely, however, all the introductory courses will share a fundamental interest in critical thinking and writing, the importance of supporting claims with reasons, and a commitment to letting you think for yourself. A philosophy class is not the place to be if you're intellectually lazy, or lack curiosity, because you will be required to respond to philosophers' arguments in a rational way.

The influential eighteenth-century philosopher Immanuel Kant (1724–1804) characterized the kind of mental laziness that sometimes makes thinking for ourselves difficult as "self-imposed tutelage": a kind of slavery or dependency. He thought that the process of thinking for ourselves could release us from self-imposed tutelage. He wrote:

> Tutelage is the inability to use one's natural powers without direction from another. This tutelage is called "self-imposed" because it came about not by any absence of rational competence but simply a lack of courage and resolution to use one's reason without direction from another. *Sapere aude!*—Dare to reason! Have the courage to use your own minds!—is the motto of the enlightenment.
>
> Laziness and cowardice explain why so many ... remain under a life-long tutelage and why it is so easy for some ... to set themselves up as the guardians of all the rest.... If I have a book which understands for me, a pastor who has a conscience for me, a doctor who decides my diet, I need not trouble myself. If I am willing to pay, I need not think. Others will do it for me.

Your philosophy instructor will almost certainly be an enemy of self-imposed tutelage.

Philosophy instructors vary in the emphasis they put on factual and historical information, but as a rule philosophy courses do not stress either names and dates to the extent a history course might or facts and terms the way a geography course can. Still, you cannot critically consider an issue if you do not memorize some basic information, whether it be historical, technical, or the meanings of key terms and concepts.

ACQUIRING INFORMED OPINIONS

Most students already have opinions about many of the topics covered in philosophy courses, although very few students have had the opportunity to analyze and justify these opinions in the sustained, critical way that's common to most philosophy classes. One of the things you can expect to study in a philosophy course is the difference between *uninformed opinion* (often called "mere opinion") and *informed opinion*.

A common misconception about philosophy is that it's just one philosopher's opinion versus another philosopher's opinion. This idea rests on a fundamental confusion about the different levels of justification. "Mere belief" is the conviction that something is true based solely on the sincere conviction of the believer that it is true. A tiny, inadequate step up from mere belief is uninformed opinion, based on vague notions, common prejudices, and a variety of inexpert sources, such as the mass media or individuals speaking out on issues they have not subjected to careful, critical, study.

Today's cultural climate is pretty hostile to informed, critical opinion: it doesn't make good sound bites on the evening news, nor is it compatible with blind allegiance to a political party, social doctrine, or any strong belief. Television talk shows inundate us with shouting, belligerent, "sincere" advocates for all sorts of beliefs. What they rarely present—or tolerate—is the care necessary for thoughtful reflection and analysis of these often very important issues. Certainly, most advertisers, and many politicians and social reformers, don't want you to think for yourself; they want your agreement, allegiance, or financial support.

Your philosophy instructor will help you develop some thinking skills that can free you from self-imposed, media-imposed, even friends-and-family-imposed tutelage. Thinking for yourself is like walking, running, or lifting for yourself; it's more difficult than letting someone else do it, but it's also much more satisfying. It's psychologically satisfying because skills mastery is intrinsically pleasing, and it's liberating because you are in the driver's seat when you think for yourself.

Expect your instructor to demand that you present reasons to support your opinions with rigor and clarity. Don't despair. She or he is there to teach you how to meet a higher standard of proof, not to show up your faults or cut you down. The only way to learn how to present good reasons is by recognizing bad—or nonexistent—ones, especially when they're your own.

A common method of teaching philosophy involves deliberately challenging your present beliefs—not because they are necessarily unsupportable, but to help you see just how sound they are. It can be quite discouraging to discover that you can't support some of your most cherished beliefs. It can also be quite exciting to discover that you *can*. In either case, your instructor is likely to be more concerned with helping you learn how to think philosophically than with teaching you what to think. This can be initially frustrating if you're used to being told "the truth" by authority figures. But once you experience the excitement of challenging important ideas, "deliberate philosophical tension" will become quite stimulating.

The combination of sometimes controversial, often abstract, topics and the introduction of new standards of proof can confuse new philosophy students. Stick with it. Work at refining your thinking skills, and frustration will turn to interest and possibly even enchantment. You'll take justifiable pride in your more polished thinking.

SPECIAL FEATURES OF PHILOSOPHY COURSES

- Philosophy courses devote considerable attention to reasons and arguments. Precision and clarity are highly valued.

- Students (and instructors) are expected to defend interpretations and positions rationally.

- Many philosophical arguments are complex and abstract.

- Equally compelling reasons often support conflicting points of view.

- The topics studied in philosophy courses often challenge or directly reject commonly held opinions.

- Philosophy instructors often place as much (if not more) emphasis on the reasoning offered for a position as they do on "getting the right answer."

- Many (if not most) of the philosophies covered will seem persuasive and flawed at the same time. (That's because they are.)

- Philosophy has been characterized as the art of questioning. Philosophy courses can be frustrating to students used to getting "the correct answer."

- No philosophical idea or value is sacred. Any philosophical position worth holding is a fair subject for critical analysis.

GETTING THE MOST OUT OF A PHILOSOPHY (OR ANY) CLASS

- **Develop a mature attitude.** Give all ideas a fair initial hearing, even if you can't imagine holding them yourself. Don't "shoot from the hip" and make impulsive, uninformed prejudgments.

- **Don't confuse having a strong opinion with being right.** You probably hold strong beliefs about many issues you've not recently (if ever) thoroughly and objectively analyzed.

- **Participate in class.** Volunteer to answer questions when the instructor asks them. Offer supporting examples and ask for clarification.

- **Don't immediately raise your objections to new ideas.** Make sure you understand the *entire* issue and its significance to the point being developed in class before raising objections. If you find yourself repeatedly tempted to object to "wrong" beliefs, you may be locked into a defensive attitude that will prevent you from understanding many of the things you are expected to learn. Don't try to get a good education (especially a philosophical one) and also hold on to all of your present ideas. You won't have gotten much of an education if you are the same person at graduation as you were when you began.

- **Practice the principle of charity.** In simple terms, the principle of charity directs you to begin your analysis of a passage or argument by interpreting any ambiguities and apparent inconsistencies to the advantage of the point being advanced. This will prevent you from reading with a selective bias or prejudice against a position that challenges an important belief, or that expresses a new idea. Your first careful reading of a philosophical passage should always be based on the assumption that the author's intention is to present good reasons for his or her position—and that he or she is capable of doing so. This attitude gives you the best chance of understanding the original argument. It minimizes the chances that you will distort ideas that you don't like. Psychologists who study learning report that people have the most difficulty understanding and remembering ideas they disagree with. That's not surprising. But you can use that information to help you become a better student and better thinker by consciously resisting the impulse to look for weaknesses before you fully grasp a position. (CAUTION: Do not expect your professor to read your work under the principle of charity. In order to strengthen your writing and thinking skills, your instructor will probably interpret gaps, inconsistencies, and ambiguities as errors on your part. Always hold yourself to a high standard of expression and proof, just to be safe.)

- **Think in terms of understanding rather than judging.** Reread the preceding tip.

- **Continually ask yourself why you believe X and not Y.**

- **Don't settle for superficial, easy answers.**

- **Work, work, work.** Accept the fact that to understand what's going on in class you'll need to read your assignments on time, and you'll most likely need to reread them once or twice.

- **Read, read, and reread.** There is no substitute for carefully reading all assignments. The more you read, the better you read and the more you learn.

- **Come to class with questions and ask them.** IMPORTANT NOTE: You'll be much more confident about asking questions if you come to class prepared. It's especially difficult to ask questions if you're not sure what's in the reading assignment. Writing down a question often triggers the answer to it or clarifies the problem in a way that indicates what's needed to get an answer.

- **If a point made in lecture is unclear, wait a few minutes to see whether subsequent remarks clear it up. If not, ask for clarification.** If you cannot bring yourself to ask questions during class, make a specific note of your confusion. After class, write your question neatly, and give it to your instructor before the next lecture. Meanwhile, study the issue on your own, and, if necessary, modify your notes.

- **Ask for clarification of all assignments when they are made.** Don't ever leave class without being very sure you understand all assignments.

- **Follow instructions.** Don't make any modification without specific permission from your instructor.

- **Exchange phone numbers with at least one other class member, and agree to share notes and information when one of you is absent.** (To abuse this agreement is to risk destroying it.)

- **Always take your book to class.** You never know when it will come in handy.

- **Sit up front, toward the center.** Studies indicate that where you sit can affect your performance in class. If you sit near the instructor, you'll feel more involved in class. It's more difficult to daydream and doze off right under the professor's nose. From a statistical point of view, the most academically dangerous seats are those that create a sense of distance and anonymity—far back, rear sides, the obscure middle of large lecture halls, and so forth.

DECIDING WHAT IS NOTEWORTHY

- **Always come to class prepared to take notes.** You'll certainly want to note important due dates, changes in the assignment schedule, and so forth, in addition to lecture notes.

- **Be spacious.** Bring a generous supply of paper to class so that you can allow plenty of space between key words and phrases in your notes. If you use lined paper, skip two or three lines between each distinct idea, argument, issue, term, and so forth. When you review your notes, you can add clarifying details from the textbook, dictionaries, and study sessions with other students. You may find it helpful to make two columns for notes, one for basic lecture information, and the other to be used when adding clarifying details later.

- **Gear your notes to your instructor's teaching style as follows:**

  Lectures that repeat the text. Some instructors prefer to follow the text closely in their lectures. In that case, you won't need to take very thorough notes regarding the information conveyed in class. You'll probably do best by *not* trying to transcribe every name, date, definition, and idea mentioned in class (you can look them up in the text). Instead, listen carefully for new insights or alternative explanations of complex ideas. Make note of them—use key phrases that will remind you of examples, analogies, or simplified definitions when you review and flesh out your notes later (as, of course, you will do).

  Lectures that convey information not found in text. If your instructor's lectures contain a wealth of new information, you will need to take careful, thorough notes. You might consider developing your own form of shorthand. If you do, be consistent. For example, many people use "w/" to mean *with* and "@" to mean *according to*, and so forth.

  Lectures that consist of wide-ranging elaborations on key ideas but do not repeat or strictly follow the text. Don't attempt to record such lectures verbatim, and don't attempt to organize their content as you take notes. Some of the best lecturers are the most difficult to take notes from because their lectures have a life of their own. No two lectures on Socrates, for instance, are ever the same for some spell-binding master-lecturers. Don't be frustrated. Relax and "go with the flow." Listen actively. Respond spontaneously with your own inner dialogue. Record useful bits and pieces from your reactions, using key phrases. You cannot (and need not) take exhaustive, conventional notes from some lecturers. In most cases of this nature, the purpose of the lecture is to involve you in the *philosophical process* (called "doing philosophy"). Your instructor probably expects you to get detailed information from the text. Such "demonstration" lectures expose you to philosophy in practice. They are designed to inspire you, not to duplicate the text.

- **Record all new and/or complex information and ideas.**
  Don't assume that you'll be able to remember what you hear in
  class. There simply may be too many new ideas for that to be possible. Further, you will need time to distill new ideas. Take notes
  that will enable you to concentrate on relationships and connections among ideas. Copy all alternative definitions and explanations for technical terms. Record illustrative examples.

- **Don't try to take notes word for word.** Jot down key words
  and phrases, and make diagrams.

- **Record all charts, definitions, and outlines from the board
  or overhead projections (if they are not from the text).**

- **Take special care to record** *every idea you dislike.* Cognitive
  scientists have shown that we tend to overlook, forget, or distort
  ideas that challenge or seriously disagree with our most important
  desires and fundamental beliefs. We tend to trivialize and un-
  consciously alter opposing ideas to make them less threatening.
  Unpleasant and threatening ideas are also more difficult to understand, so you'll need to put special effort into recording them accurately and completely—and into studying them later.

- **Be very careful to include all modifiers and qualifying
  terms.** Words like *always, sometimes, probably, might, never,* and the
  like are crucial parts of claims. Leaving them out significantly
  changes the meaning of the original idea. For example, changing
  "Philosophy and religion sometimes overlap" to "Philosophy and
  religion overlap" changes the meaning of the original sentence.

- **Ask questions and make comments as part of your notes.**
  Keep track of any questions (or strong reactions) you have to ideas
  expressed in class. Use a "?" to mean why? Be brief but clear.
  "Proof?" can mean "How does X know? What's the evidence?" A
  "!" can mean *great!* or *wow!* Use "N" for *no* and "Y" for *yes* to indicate agreement or disagreement. Use "NB" from the Latin *nota
  bene* for *note well* or *pay attention.*

- **Polish your notes soon after you take them.** Go over your
  notes the same day you make them. Try to make a quick polish
  within an hour or so after you've taken your notes. Fill in details.
  Restate cloudy passages. Use the generous spaces you left to am-
  plify your necessarily incomplete notes.

WHY ATTENDANCE MATTERS

- **Studying philosophy is a skill and a way of thinking, in addition to being a set of key issues and individuals.** You'll need to experience the way your instructor "does philosophy" on a regular basis if you want to do more than just acquire philosophical information.

- **You're more likely to learn if you feel safe and comfortable, and you're more likely to feel safe and comfortable if you know what's going on.** Instructors often modify schedules, announce extensions for assignments, and so forth in class. You'll want to get this useful information right away.

- **Getting to know and recognize classmates, no matter how casually, will enhance your sense of belonging.** You'll be more able to discuss course material and share common frustrations before and after class if you're on friendly terms with other students. Every little bit of anxiety reduction helps.

- **Attending class regularly keeps philosophical issues at the forefront of your mind.** Not all learning is deliberate and conscious. Listening to your instructor's explanations and elaborations of textual material can trigger new connections for you, spark your own creative ideas, and identify areas of misunderstanding.

- **You can benefit by others' questions and by following student-instructor interchanges.**

- **You're likely to improve your understanding of assigned readings after your instructor has discussed them in class.** Don't rob yourself of this vital resource.

- **When an instructor says that "attendance does not count," that only refers to his or her grading policy. Attendance always affects learning.**

- **Whether or not you get specific credit toward a grade for attendance, most instructors are favorably impressed by regular, *attentive* attendance.** Assigning grades is a complex process, and the difference between a B– and C+ might be your instructor's unconscious sense of your class participation or attendance. (It is reasonable for instructors to conclude that students cannot have learned material covered in their absence, and thus not award the higher of two possible grades to those with significant absences.)

- **Instructors need regular feedback from students.** Most instructors modify their courses according to student response. Students' body language, comments, and questions are vital clues for gearing a lecture's content and pace to its audience. The reactions of students who just drop in now and then are not reliable indicators of a course's effectiveness.

WHY ETHICAL BEHAVIOR MATTERS

Everyone benefits from a pleasant classroom atmosphere. An essential component of a good learning environment is mutual respect. Instructors and students are equally entitled to courteous, respectful treatment from each other. Therefore, you have special responsibilities and obligations as a student. (Instructors also have special ethical obligations, but this is a student manual so we won't address that issue here.)

The following list of guidelines rests on the premise that ethical behavior has both moral and practical benefits. In other words, it is to your personal advantage to behave ethically.

- **Be courteous in class.** Disrupting class robs other students and your instructor of their time. It may also draw the kind of attention to you that negatively affects your grades.

- **Don't cheat in any form.** Cheating is a form of theft. If cheating is widespread, it leads to general contempt for education. If very many people get good grades they have not earned, the value of everyone's grade point average (and degree) is diminished. The more mediocre, marginally qualified, semiliterate college graduates there are, the less significance your degree will have.

- **Keep your commitments.** Your instructor has to budget his or her time, too. When you turn in papers late or ask to take tests late, you place extra demands on that time. Be sure you have very good reasons before doing so.

- **If you can't resist communicating with your friends during class, don't sit near them.** All discussion in class should relate to the class and be directed to the entire class (unless your instructor assigns you to small groups). Fidgeting, mumbling, or passing notes interferes with the concentration of others and deprives them of their very basic right to a congenial learning environment.

- **Arrive on time and remain for the entire period, unless you've made other arrangements with your instructor.** Wandering in and out of class on your own schedule cheapens the atmosphere of the course. Such conduct suggests indifference, if not contempt, for what's happening in class. Leaving in the middle of class is like walking away without explanation in the middle of a conversation—not a respectful or friendly thing to do. Making the effort to arrive on time is another way of reinforcing the message to yourself that your classes and degree are important to you.

- **Don't show off.** Most of us are familiar with the student-as-star. This is the individual who has plenty to say at every class meeting. When one or two students dominate class time, the rest of the class grows resentful and may tune out whenever the student-as-star has the floor. It's best to avoid the extremes of excessive shyness and excessive demands for attention. Give less confident students a chance to partake in class discussions.

- **Don't ask foolish questions.** The old saying notwithstanding, there *are* foolish questions. Don't use class time to ask any question you can find the answer to by yourself. Don't ask questions if you have not been studying, because you won't have any idea whether or not the answers are in the reading. When you ask foolish questions, you steal time from others.

- **Don't sign up for high-demand classes unless you are reasonably sure you will complete them.** Many colleges today suffer from overcrowding. When an important class is closed, students who need that class may find themselves forced to take less desirable alternatives or attend an extra term. If you drop out of such a class after the enrollment period is over, you've essentially wasted a valuable opportunity and prevented anyone else from taking advantage of it. Dropping a class is not merely a personal matter.

- **Treat student evaluations with care.** Though you may not be aware of it, most instructors react to student evaluations. If a number of students praise a feature of the class, instructors are likely to continue it. If a number of students complain about the same thing, most instructors take it seriously. Student evaluations are your chance to help your instructor and his or her future students. If you have complaints, present them in a mature manner. Personal attacks and X-rated language tend to be dismissed as the immature reactions of failing students. Be specific. State what is good or bad about the course and why.

CHAPTER 2

Reading Philosophy

Most philosophical literature attempts to make a rational case that will support a philosophical point of view. Even when philosophical literature is emotionally powerful, creative, and witty, aesthetic qualities take second place to the presentation of a philosophical argument.

As a rule, philosophers attempt to present a tightly reasoned chain of ideas leading from basic, initially clear ideas to less obvious, more complex ones. One consequence of this noble goal is that reading philosophical literature requires a high level of patience and concentration. Because important points are connected to specific preceding points, it's important not to lose track of the line of reasoning. This takes effort and close concentration.

Philosophers often invent their own technical vocabulary in an attempt to be both clear and fair. Sometimes philosophers coin brand new words; other times they give their own special meanings to words already in use. *Failure to note the precise meaning of key terms results in failure to follow the philosopher's line of reasoning.* Keeping track of these technical meanings can be difficult, but it cannot be avoided. Not all philosophers are careful to define the unique meanings of key terms. Philosophical readers must always be on the lookout for unusual uses of common terms as well as for newly coined terms.

Sometimes, philosophers even use the same term to mean different things without warning the reader. *In addition to watching for the meaning of key terms, you must check to see that terms retain a consistent meaning.*

HEALTHY CONFUSION

Don't be surprised if your first reading of a philosophical text confuses you. I find that I must read most philosophical arguments at least twice, and often three times, before I really begin to understand them.

When you find yourself confused and frustrated, remember that you are learning a new technical vocabulary as well as trying to identify a line of reasoning that may involve sidelines and subpoints. This requires a form of mental juggling. You must retain a number of isolated pieces of information until you can identify the overall structure of the argument.

Don't be surprised or intimidated if you initially feel confused by philosophy. Most of that confusion clears up if you merely persist, being as attentive as possible at each reading. You will often find that after a few pages of difficulty, your comprehension suddenly improves. When that happens, it's a good idea to go back and immediately reread preceding relevant material.

QUICK TIPS FOR MORE EFFECTIVE READING

Here's a list of techniques and strategies that help many readers. Feel free to modify them according to your own reading experience. If, however, you find reading abstract or complex material difficult, or if such material is new to you, it's probably a good idea to give these tips a try.

- **Always skim to get an overview.** Skim the table of contents of the book (or the headings in a chapter). Flip through articles, chapters, or sections using headings and subheadings to get a sense of organizational structure. Read the preface or introductory notes provided by the editor or author. Check to see whether there is an index and glossary.

- **Begin with a general idea of the passage's main point and its strategy for establishing that point.** You can get this information from chapter summaries, from your instructor, and from other books and articles. (See the "Beginning Philosopher's Bibliography" at the end of this manual.)

- **Read with a pencil, highlighter, or pad of stick-it notes handy, and flag technical terms and important passages as you come across them.**

- **Read in good light.**

- **Find a comfortable spot away from distractions.** Some people study better with a little background music, others don't. Do what works for you. Pick a study spot that's good for your needs, and study in the same spot whenever possible.

- **Make reading a priority.** If you become distracted by thoughts of other things you need to do, write them down to deal with after you are through reading. *Then,* tell yourself that this is your time to read. Stay focused on reading.

- **Suspend personal judgments and don't forget the principle of charity (see "Getting the Most Out of a Philosophy (or Any) Class," p. 12).** Completely ignore whether or not you like what is being claimed. Your initial readings should be only for comprehension. Evaluation should come later, because critical evaluation depends on clearly understanding what is being claimed and how that claim is being supported.

- **Use the glossary and a good unabridged dictionary.** Look up difficult words right away.

- **Consider buying a philosophical dictionary.** General reference dictionaries do not contain *technical* definitions of philosophical terms.

- **Read through an entire section in one sitting, even if you don't understand most of it.** After your first reading, you'll have a clearer idea of the structure of the argument or explanation. You'll be in good shape to reread more closely. You'll understand much more on the second reading because you know how points made in one part of the passage relate to points made elsewhere. You'll also know what's most important and why.

- **Take regular breaks that are long enough to clear your mind and give your eyes a rest.** Stop reading often enough to prevent fatigue. Don't consciously think about what you've just read. Move around, stretch. Allow your unconscious mind to process the material.

- **Reread as often as *you* need to.** Don't fall into the trap of comparing your study needs to others.

- **Vary your reading speed.** As a general rule, you need to read important, technically difficult passages at a slower rate than less complex informational passages.

- **Pause regularly to see whether you can clearly restate difficult passages in your own words.** Don't just assume that you understand something because you're not having any noticeable trouble reading it. Forcing yourself to restate important ideas at regular intervals is an effective way of testing comprehension.

- **Reread difficult passages in a different way.** You may find that you have to take one sentence at a time when reading especially complex or poorly written technical passages. You may need to look up the meanings of two or three words in one paragraph. *Whatever you do, don't merely repeat the kind of reading that's not working.*

- **When you're in a rut, flag and skip unusually resistant passages; return to them later.** Don't spend so much time and effort on one difficult passage that you get completely confused, frustrated, and dispirited. If careful rereading isn't working, continue with the rest of the chapter. This often clarifies the difficult passage.

- **Ask your instructor to recommend some supplementary reading for especially resistant passages.** If the preceding tip doesn't work, consult another text that deals with the same point. Sometimes just reading a different explanation will clear things up. There are many excellent philosophy textbooks and reference books available.

- **Don't confuse a tired mind or body with reading difficulties.** If everything you're reading suddenly makes no sense, or you encounter an especially difficult passage at the end of a long day or study session, you may just be too tired to benefit from more work. Get some rest.

- **Perform routine maintenance.** Don't get too hungry, thirsty, or tired. Avoid all alcohol and drugs, because drugs and alcohol inhibit comprehension skills.

- **After you've given all these tips a fair try, ask your instructor for additional help.** Sometimes one more clarification or explanation is all it takes to unlock the meaning of a difficult passage.

- **Make sure you don't have a reading or comprehension problem.** If you are having reading difficulties in most of your classes, consult a counselor. There are simple, free tests your school can provide that can identify common, *manageable* reading and comprehension difficulties.

- **If your counselor or instructor recommends the college reading lab, take advantage of its tutorial services.** Don't be too embarrassed to get help if you need it. The staff of the reading lab is there to help you succeed on your own. Staff members will not embarrass you or make you dependent on them. Think of them as fulfilling a function similar to that of a good physical trainer. You will do all the work and earn all the credit; they will help you develop better skills.

BEYOND THE TEXTBOOK

Although your textbook is probably your primary source of detailed information, it is not your only source. Develop the habit of taking full advantage of all appropriate resources. Become a study artisan, using a full set of special tools.

- **Use this book!** Hang on to *How to Get the Most Out of Philosophy, Second Edition,* and review it when you need a basic study pep talk or a little friendly encouragement.

- **Maximize your use of your philosophy textbook.** Use all of its pedagogical (effective teaching and learning) features: chapter introductions, summaries, study questions, glossaries, index, chapter headings, and so forth.

- **Take advantage of any study guides or student manuals available for your textbook, or prepared and distributed by your instructor.** Don't be too "hip" or "cool" to use these features. Among their advantages, four stand out: (1) They *focus your attention* on key ideas, figures, and so forth. (2) They require *active reading*. (3) They involve *repetition*. (4) The best study guides involve *written responses*.

- **Regularly check your comprehension by writing down your own summary of a section's key points and arguments in your own words.** Check your summary against the text. If you can accurately and thoroughly summarize a position, you understand it. *If you cannot accurately and thoroughly summarize a position, you do not understand it.* Period. This is the best self-test you can perform for comprehension. It's important because, as you know, you cannot analyze or evaluate an idea until you can understand it without distorting it.

- **Ask your friends to grade your summaries (see preceding tip), and offer to grade theirs.** This exercise is another opportunity for *active reading and thinking*. It develops concentration and comprehension.

- **Discuss the reading material with others.** One of the best ways of testing comprehension is by refining your understanding of an idea or argument by verbally expressing it in your own words to someone else.

- **Use the library.** Most college libraries have copies of the *Encyclopedia of Philosophy* and a variety of philosophical history books and commentaries, as well as other philosophy textbooks. Ask your instructor for recommended supplemental reading. It's also a good idea to just browse through the philosophy stacks (section of shelves). If you try reading two or three different authors' treatments of the same issues, you'll probably find they're each especially helpful in different ways.

- **Consult reference and technical sources.** See the "Beginning Philosopher's Bibliography" at the end of this book, and consult the bibliography of your textbook for the names of good reference books. Talk to your college library's reference librarian.

PART TWO

Critical Thinking, Reading, And Writing

Perhaps the most valuable product of a good education is the development of a critical attitude. In this context, *critical* does not mean negative or hostile. From the Greek root *kritikes*, meaning "to judge" or "to discern," a critical attitude is one that does not take things at face value, and that demands reasonable proof before accepting or rejecting claims.

The heart of a critical attitude is sophisticated, rational analysis of truth claims, whether they occur in formal philosophical arguments, political speeches, sermons, commercials, contracts, or in everyday conversation.

Developing a healthy critical attitude is an important function of any philosophy course. Initially, your instructor's demand for critical responses can be frustrating, especially if you have not had much practice carefully analyzing and justifying your opinions by making a rational case for them. But critical thinking, reading, and writing are vital student skills that can be developed and polished like many other skills.

Chapter 3 is a basic overview of critical thinking. Chapters 4 and 5 apply critical thinking skills and principles to reading and writing.

CHAPTER 3

Developing A Critical Attitude

The term *critical thinking* is widely used in educational circles. You're probably already familiar with it. Here is a list of some of the chief characteristics of critical thinking:

- **Critical thinking is the conscious, deliberate, rational assessment of claims according to clearly identified standards of proof.** Although appropriate standards of proof vary, depending on the nature of the claim, certain fundamental principles of reasoning apply to all critical thinking. These include standards of relevance, consistency, reasonableness (likely to be true), and sufficiency. Any claim that rests on inconsistent evidence, inconsistencies between premises and their conclusions, circularity, or ambiguity must be recast or rejected.

- **Critical thinking is objective and impersonal, while recognizing that personal experience and emotion play a part in the thoughtful assessment of claims.** Critical thinking is *impersonal* in the sense that mathematics is impersonal. The truth of the sentence "2 + 2 = 4" is not a function of some particular person's moods, values, religion, gender, race, or such. The logical correctness of this pattern of reasoning is similarly *impersonal*:

> If A is greater than B, and
> If B is greater than C, and
> If C is greater than D, then
> A is greater than D.

- **Critical thinking offers sustained argumentation (verifiable, rational evidence) for claims supported by logical reasoning, expert testimony, language analysis, and appropriate personal and professional experience.** Good critical thinking presents a chain of reasons that will allow any interested, rational person to follow the evidence step by step to a rationally sustainable conclusion. Critical thinkers provide "whys" as well as "whats." That is, they explain why a position is worth holding or should be rejected in a fashion that allows others to complete a common reasoning process. This element is sometimes referred to as the *public dimension of argument.* All that means is that the process used to arrive at the conclusion is not mysterious or secret; it is subject to public scrutiny or public verification in much the same way that scientific experiments are presented in a way that enables other scientists to verify them. Basic critical thinking skills are the foundation of more specialized forms of logical analysis, scientific, or technical thinking. Basic critical thinking skills are useful in all walks of life and are one of our best defenses against self-imposed tutelage, blind prejudice, and avoidably foolish life choices.

- **Critical thinking involves *rational discourse*—the use of reason to order, clarify, identify, and articulate our basic views of reality and truth according to agreed-upon standards of evidence.** The ancient Greek philosopher Socrates (c. 470–399 B.C.) gave his name to one famous form of rational discourse known as the *Socratic method.* Many philosophy professors, and most law schools, use the Socratic method of teaching to foster critical thinking abilities in their students. This is a question-and-answer technique in which the teacher uses guided, sometimes pointed, questions that require the pupil to reason out appropriate answers.

The Socratic method demands more than just the retention and regurgitation of information; it requires the critical analysis of opinions by carefully defining key terms, drawing inferences, identifying key principles, patterns, and connections, and so forth. Socrates thought that it was very important that the pursuit of truth be public and social so that each participant could function as a monitor for other participants. In that way, our individual blind spots could be recognized and filled in by others. In my opinion, one of the most optimistic and charming aspects of Socrates was his insistence that no matter what conclusion was reached by this process (and often the conclusion was that, so far, nobody is completely correct), everyone benefited—especially those whose errors are identified. Socrates thought that the wise (rational) person will be grateful to anyone who improves his or her thinking. In other words, Socrates was more interested in getting closer to the truth than he was in his image or ego. From his perspective, rational discourse is a social good, and all true patriots participate in it, because a healthy democracy depends on enlightened citizens. If that's true, then good critical thinking skills are to everyone's advantage.

- **Critical thinking is coherent, following the evidence where it leads, in an orderly manner.** One of the signs of good critical thinking is the willingness to accept the best evidence, even when it requires modifying or rejecting a cherished belief or highly desired conclusion. As this is being written, the O. J. Simpson case is about to be brought to trial. During the countless discussions of this famous case, many legal experts have publicly expressed concern over what one of them characterized as a "growing, serious lack of rationality" among jurors in all parts of the country. Both prosecutors and defense lawyers have expressed concern over jurors who willfully disregard evidence and legally binding instructions, choosing to vote with their feelings or instincts. The issue here is not just whether a juror's vote is "correct" but whether a blatant indifference to clearly articulated reasons interferes with the process of *deliberation*, the rational assessment of evidence through forthright discussion and civil argumentation. In other words, a growing number of practicing lawyers are reporting their fears that many of our fellow citizens either cannot or will not engage in the give-and-take of reasons. Such individuals are uncritical thinkers, willing to make serious choices without taking the time, or exerting the effort, to evaluate all sides of an issue critically.

WHAT IS UNCRITICAL THINKING?

- **Uncritical thinking is characterized by lack of precision and coherence.** Students sometimes reveal poor critical thinking skills when they rely on vague claims to sustain their arguments. Basic ways to be precise include using correct technical terms and examples found in your reading, and writing short, clearly focused sentences. It also helps to avoid pontificating, or using pretentious language. If you are not comfortable reading a sentence out loud, it may be because it's unclear.

- **Uncritical thinking accepts or rejects claims according to momentary impulses, unquestioned loyalties, and unreflective personal bias.** Examples of this kind of "pseudo-thinking" abound. Consider just two typical examples from the the late summer of 1994. Before the trial even began, many people had made up their minds about whether or not O. J. Simpson was guilty of murdering his ex-wife and her friend. These people's positions were based only on newspaper, magazine, and television reports. A woman on a television talk show stated that she was convinced that Simpson was guilty because she had been battered by her ex-husband, and she "could just tell that he's guilty. I know what those guys are like. I lived with one for four years." On another show, a celebrity stated, "There's no way someone in O. J.'s position could ever do something like that. People on that level don't stab people." These comments, and others like them, were uttered with apparent sincerity. They were offered as "evidence," or reasons why these people thought as they did.

- **Uncritical thinking substitutes strong feelings for clearly stated evidence.** Whether you're a television fan or not, you've probably seen enough talk shows to recognize how commonly volume and aggressiveness substitute for rational discourse.

Guests and invited "experts" shout each other down, all talk at once, sneer, point, gesture wildly—none of which have any bearing on having a good point. Even if these methods "work" in the sense of persuading lots of people, they do not get us closer to the truth. As if that weren't bad enough, these substitutes for civilized, rational discourse probably breed cynicism and hostility. Advertisers and campaigning politicians can also assault us with uncritical, emotionally powerful substitutes for good reasons.

- **Uncritical thinking is inappropriately defensive, reacting to all criticism in a uniform fashion.** Watch for this one; it makes it very difficult to accept criticism. Even if your critic makes good points, you might be tempted to defend your ego, to "save face," by going on the attack. One common strategy here is to zero in on the critic's faults or to identify ulterior motives or ill will behind the criticism. Your position cannot, however, be strengthened by pointing out flaws in someone else, questioning their motives, and so forth.

- **Uncritical thinking confuses winning debates and popularity with being right.** Because we are such a results-oriented society, it's tempting to reduce all considerations to "Does it work?" Thus, we're tempted to admire the sleazy trick that sways the jury and overlook the fact that our legal system suffers as we become convinced that it's all just an elaborate game. Your philosophy instructor is not going to be like most people. He or she has devoted years to the study of careful reasoning, logic, critical thinking, methods of persuasion, and so forth. What looked pretty clever in a presidential debate or on the Oprah Winfrey or Phil Donahue show may not work at all in your philosophy class.

- **Uncritical thinking is sometimes impulsive, based on instantaneous judgments strongly influenced by personality, race, gender, religion, political affiliation, or deeply felt psychological needs.** We've all seen other people behave this way. Sometimes, you can almost see a kind of screen fall over their faces, indicating that nothing anyone says or does will get them to reconsider their position. When people are in this state, they are not rational; that is, reasons have no effect on their point of view.

- **Uncritical thinking confuses *willed ignorance* with *knowledgeable confidence*.** Willed ignorance is an attitude of indifference to the possibility of error or enlightenment. Willed ignorance holds on to beliefs regardless of the facts. You can recognize willed ignorance by such expressions as: "I don't care what anybody says, I know _____." "Nothing anybody says will ever change my mind about _____." "You might be right, but I don't care. I'm going to believe _____." People in the throes of willed ignorance refuse to read the literature of their opponents: "No, I've never taken any courses in evolution, I don't have to. I just know those scientists are wrong." "I've never listened to Rush Limbaugh, because he's a bigot." In a nutshell, willed ignorance is unresponsive to reasons, facts, and evidence that challenge preferred points of view.

WHAT DOES CRITICAL THINKING REQUIRE?

- **Critical thinking requires the application of appropriate standards of evidence.** What counts as adequate evidence in an informal conversation will probably not be adequate for a philosophy class discussion. Similarly, what's adequate for a class discussion will not be adequate for an essay or term paper.

- **Critical thinking requires intellectual maturity.** Good critical thinkers do not allow their feelings and personal preferences to control their judgment. When criticized, the critical thinker always asks; "Is this criticism valid?" If it is, she modifies her original position, since her goal is truth, not mere face-saving.

- **Critical thinking takes *work*.** Important issues require careful study. You cannot make reasonable decisions if you do not study issues for yourself—all you can do is react based on partial, second-hand opinions and untested beliefs and prejudices.

- **Critical thinking requires practice.** Athletes and artists have to work regularly to maintain a certain level of proficiency. Critical thinking skills also require regular exercise.

- **Critical thinking requires courage.** It can be difficult to ask, "How do you know that?" People sometimes resent being asked to prove their claims. They may be insulted if we don't just accept what they say because they're our friends or relatives. They may be defensive because our questions reveal that they don't have good reasons for their assertions. Sometimes people don't have *any* reasons for their assertions.

- **Critical thinking requires tact.** Because we depend on one another in our search for truth, it's always best to avoid asking questions in a way that's likely to turn discussions into personal disputes. Angry exchanges reduce, rather than enlarge, our fund of information. The most effective critical thinkers do not shy away from asking necessary questions or pointing out important errors, but they do so with respect and courtesy, fully aware that they might be wrong themselves. As a very general rule, people tend to respond better to clearheaded, focused assertiveness than to self-righteous aggression or unshakeable willed ignorance.

CRITICAL THINKING PRACTICES THAT PAY OFF IN THE CLASSROOM AND BEYOND

- **Distinguish what is important from what is not according to regularly reevaluated principles.** Just as it is unwise to treat important issues as matters of mere preference, it is unwise to subject all issues to a single, excessively detailed analysis. *Hairsplitting* is the name some philosophers give to the error of uncritically excessive analysis of minor points, as if they were major ones. By distinguishing what is important from what is not, good critical thinkers don't get bogged down in a quagmire of tedious minutiae.

- **Pay careful attention to the meanings of terms.** Philosophy is a language-intensive subject. Complex ideas and complex arguments are basic to most philosophical (and all sophisticated) writing. Philosophy, like most academic subjects, has its own technical vocabulary. Many of these technical terms are based on non-English roots. Here are some examples of technical philosophical language: dialectic, noumena, phenomena, a priori, a posteriori, eudaimonia, entelechy, mystification, contradiction, ontological, valid, circular, tautology. You are not unintelligent if you do not know what they mean. You are *ignorant* in the sense of simply lacking experience and knowledge of these terms. You certainly wouldn't try to take a French test without learning some French. If you don't speak French, there is one sense in which you "don't know" what it means to say, "*La plume de ma tante est sur la table.*" Once you make the translation to "My aunt's pen is on the table," everything clears up. The concept is readily understood once the language is understood.

- **Be sure you understand exactly what is being said before you do anything else.** One of the most common mistakes students make is trying to evaluate a claim without first understanding exactly what is being said. For instance, one semester a student came by my office and said, "I'm having trouble understanding what Aristotle means by *eudaimonia*." "All right," I said, "why don't you just tell me what the word *eudaimonia* means." "That's the problem!" he exclaimed. "I can't understand what Aristotle means." "How could you," I asked, "if you have no idea whatsoever what this key word means?" I sent the student away with specific pages to read in our textbook (pages that had been assigned over a week earlier) that included a definition and explanation of *eudaimonia*—which, incidentally, is a term Aristotle used to refer to a fully realized existence, a state of being fully aware, vital, and alert. (It is often translated as *happiness,* but "happiness" is probably too restrictive for the fullness Aristotle had in mind.) If my student had said, "I'm not sure what it means to be 'fully realized'," I could have helped him. But he had not done his homework, literally and figuratively. The bottom line is that critical thinking is always about something: terms, facts, causal claims, and so forth. There is no shortcut through memorizing and understanding. (Oh yes, after reading the material with attentiveness and care, my student had no trouble understanding *eudaimonia* well enough to write a clear essay commenting on Aristotle's conception of happiness.) Don't confuse being poorly prepared with an inability to understand.

- **Rely on relevant expertise when appropriate.** No one can possess significant knowledge of all the kinds of issues that confront people. Socrates insisted that the search for truth cannot begin until we honestly acknowledge the limits of our own knowledge. You can maximize your critical thinking efforts by taking advantage of the accumulated knowledge of experts. Just be sure that any experts you consult possess expertise in the field in question and that most other qualified experts agree with them. Even if you do not know the particulars of a given subject area, you can still apply careful thought to selecting the experts you rely on.

- **Question any claim that is fundamentally inconsistent with your own carefully evaluated experience (including claims from experts).** I keep a file of deceptive and bogus advertisements. One of my favorites is a flyer for a book of "exam secrets" that *guarantees* a "great GPA" with no effort. I don't know about your experience, but I've never seen anything capable of *guaranteeing* a great GPA. Don't you think such a "secret" would sweep the nation—no, sweep the world? The same is true for hair restorers, 200-mile-per-gallon gadgets to add to your car, and $50 Rolex watches for sale in the cafeteria.

- **Analyze the motives of all interested parties (including your own), without reducing critical scrutiny to character analysis.** Contrary to common opinion, a person's intentions or motives do not tell us much about the reliability of their claims and arguments. When you uncover hidden biases or ulterior motives, you have an additional reason to scrutinize a claimant's assertions. But it is the asserted evidence that needs to be evaluated, not the arguer.

- **Distinguish between the arguer and the argument.** A variety of logical fallacies stem from confusing arguers with their arguments. Perhaps the best known is the *argumentum ad hominem,* literally "argument against the man," but now more commonly known as the *personal attack.* The most blatant form of personal attack is the *character assassination:* "You should reject the president's health care program because he has been unfaithful to his wife." A more subtle—and so more dangerous—version of the personal attack is the *circumstantial personal attack:* "We can ignore Professor Wadsworth's argument supporting a woman's right to abortion on demand. The professor's husband owns an abortion clinic." The *tu* *quoque* or *"look who's talking"* is another common form of confusing the arguer with the argument: "You're a fine one to tell me to quit smoking. You could stand to lose a few pounds." Notice that in each of these examples, the character and motives of the arguers do not of themselves have any bearing on whether or not the positions being advocated are sound. Whether or not my friend is overweight, I should rationally consider his argument against smoking. Professor Wadsworth's argument may be solid, even if the *motive* for making it is blind loyalty to her husband. The president may have unacceptable personal behavior *and at the same time* advocate a wise health plan.

- **Respect differing points of view when they are reasonably defended.** A big problem with contempt for views with which we disagree is that we close ourselves off from the opportunity to learn and grow. (I would certainly hate to think that I will not change any of my fundamental beliefs one tiny bit for the rest of my life.)

- **Encourage rational discourse by allowing those with whom you disagree to present their point of view for themselves.** This means not interrupting those whose views we abhor by shouting them down before they've finished making their point. Being "correct" is not always enough, if in the process of expressing our views we generate hostility to rational discourse or substitute verbal abuse or physical force for intelligent defense of our views. Everybody loses when issues are decided by coercion or the loudest voice.

- **Welcome legitimate criticism by remaining open to the possibility of error.** If truth is what you seek, then you need to know the weaknesses in your ideas in order to improve them or set them aside as unsalvageable. "Playing ostrich" by attempting to avoid criticism does nothing to strengthen a position. A person with cancer has cancer whether or not a doctor diagnoses cancer. Remaining in denial may prevent curing a curable condition. Refusing to consider clear, fair criticism does nothing to strengthen your own case, and it may harm your sense of self-respect. A confident truth seeker has no reason to fear criticism. A lazy or fearful thinker will, however, be afraid of anything that will require effort or serious reassessment of a cherished belief.

- **Ask important and relevant questions tactfully and at appropriate times—and wait for a complete answer.** Asking questions serves a twofold purpose: (1) The question and answer process can refine and clarify a position. (2) Asking questions and listening to answers keeps the questioner alert and mentally active.

- **Suspend judgment until *both sides* of an issue have been given a fair hearing.** This requires being genuinely open to all reasonable, relevant evidence and commits us to more than just token listening designed to create an impression of fairness. If I've already decided before you present your case, then even though I appear to be listening, I'm not really *hearing* you. Here's one more reminder to practice the principle of charity: it opens us up to a wider range of resources and improves our chances of making wise decisions.

- **Devote enough time to *research* vital issues for yourself.** Avoid relying on the mass media or authority figures for information or viewpoints. For the most part, the mass media are not reliable sources of important factual or technical information. If you want information about health care, vitamins, abortion ethics, race relations, educational patterns, and so forth, you will need to consult textbooks, professional journals, and various experts. Sales brochures put out by health food companies make claims that need to be verified against independent sources; statistics cited by pro-life and pro-choice advocates need to be checked—and so on and on. To repeat, critical thinking is an *activity*; it takes *work*.

- **Regularly remind yourself that those you disagree with believe that they are being reasonable.** Socrates thought that all evil results from ignorance. He argued that no one willingly chooses evil. I'm not sure he's completely correct, but I do think that most people want to be right, want to have good reasons. At any rate, it's probably best for us to act as if others want to be right. This humanizes our ideological opponents and reminds us that most of us are fellow travelers in the search for wisdom, truth, and happiness. More often than not, respect for others reduces stress in our own lives. Note, however, that respect for others as serious truth seekers is not the same thing as naive or gullible acceptance of every idea as plausible. Nor is respecting others an excuse not to keep looking for more truth ourselves.

- **Make a sustained effort to get information from a variety of reliable sources.** I once had a fascinating student, a very intelligent man in his mid-fifties. He was absolutely convinced that the Holocaust of World War II was a big hoax. Nothing I, nor any of his other professors, said or showed him changed his mind. He fell back on his very considerable and expensive library of history books all supporting his odd contention. This man worked hard to sustain his belief. He read literally hundreds of books—very carefully. When I pointed out that most of these books were published by six companies, three of which had the same address, he just shrugged. The moral of the story is that no quantity of biased or weak evidence suddenly becomes good evidence. One way of sustaining a position of willed ignorance is to exert precious effort in a blind cause.

THREE BASIC STANDARDS OF EVIDENCE

1. **Relevance: Evidence offered to support a claim must be directly related to establishing the truth of that claim.**

   Two examples of irrelevant evidence:

   (a) Buying a product because it is a best seller. The fact that millions of people buy X has no direct bearing on whether or not *you* should buy X.

   (b) Rejecting or accepting a claim because you don't like the person making it. The sanitary habits, moral character, religious beliefs, race, age, gender, and social status of a person are not reasons for you to reject or accept their claims.

2. **Reasonableness: Evidence offered to support a claim must be of such a nature that a disinterested rational person with relevant knowledge and expertise would accept it.**

Two examples of unreasonable claims:

(a) Claiming that the Earth is flat. In order to sustain such a belief, you must somehow account for the consensus among qualified scientific experts that the Earth is not flat. This can only be done by assuming that the vast majority of these experts are wrong, or that they are involved in a conspiracy. Both assumptions are unreasonable.

(b) Claiming that the "medical establishment" can cure cancer but won't because doctors, hospitals, and drug companies make so much money treating it. This claim is an example of the kind of conspiracy theory that flies in the face of experience. It requires that we believe that doctors and scientists would hide the discovery of a cure for cancer rather than publish it and win worldwide acclaim, an almost guaranteed Nobel prize, tons of money for research grants, and a place in medical history. Furthermore, such theories require the unreasonable assumption that thousands of people can or will keep such an important secret for years. Last, the claim reduces all members of the medical establishment to greedy, money-hungry opportunists.

3. **Sufficiency: There must be enough reasonable, relevant evidence to support the claim.**

Three examples of insufficient evidence:

(a) Drawing conclusions about members of other ethnic groups based only on your own experiences with them and what you learn from the mass media. Even the most sociable and sophisticated among us do not have enough personal experience to draw conclusions about entire ethnic groups. The mass media present images carefully selected and edited for dramatic or novelty appeal. The mass media cannot be relied on to provide a thorough, representative view of life.

(b) Deciding that philosophy is boring based on your experiences with one course. One course from one instructor is simply not sufficient to draw conclusions about a subject.

(c) The student described earlier who denied the existence of the
     Holocaust based on his extensive reading of hundreds of vol-
     umes of biased literature. By only consulting books from a
     few publishers with an axe to grind, this man in effect lim-
     ited the scope of his support. A million dollars in play money
     is not sufficient to buy one dollar's worth of apples.

Example C is both unreasonable and insufficient.

CHAPTER 4

Applying Critical Thinking Skills To Become A Better Reader

Effective readers apply critical thinking skills to what they read, taking advantage of a variety of clues and strategies that simplify the process of understanding and evaluating different kinds of writing.

Critical reading skills can be learned and refined by most motivated readers. Philosophical writing, like most technical literature, poses special problems that can be greatly reduced by the application of a few basic principles of effective critical reading.

If you can remember lots of information about what you like, you have the basic ability to remember facts about philosophers, new technical terms, the titles of important books—and the due dates for all your assignments and tests. Even if philosophy is more difficult to read, *spending as much time* reading philosophy as reading about sports or movies or fashions will eventually make reading philosophy easier. Time and effort are important parts of ability. Critical reading skills can be developed by work.

USE YOUR TEXTBOOK'S
ORGANIZATIONAL FEATURES

- **Always read the preface.** Reading the preface is like having a little chat with the author of your textbook. The preface usually includes a brief description of the book's special features and why the author thinks they will help readers. Reading the preface will familiarize you with the author's "voice," the special style he or she has. Last, the preface may identify the author's chief goals and philosophical principles.

- **Get to know your textbook right away.** Read the table of contents. Quickly read one or two brief passages that catch your interest. Note margin quotations, boxed passages, illustrations, summaries of main points, study questions, index, and another special features designed to make the book more accessible, interesting, or understandable.

- **Take full advantage of margin quotes and boxed or offset passages.** Such features will have been carefully selected because they are especially interesting, well written, or unusual. Don't skip by them; enjoy them.

- **Familiarize yourself with the glossary (a list of definitions of key terms).** The glossary can be at the end of the text, at the beginning or end of chapters or sections, in the margins, or in some combination.

- **Study section headings.** Notice how they organize the text and provide clues about content. Text headings are like levels in an outline. In addition to labeling text sections, they classify and categorize them.

- **Before you read a chapter, review the table of contents.** If your textbook has a full table of contents, it will show the various levels of headings and subheadings in each chapter. Looking at such a table of contents is like looking at an outline. Knowing the structure of a chapter will aid in understanding its content.

- **Use section headings to organize your notes.** Some students find it helpful to list the chapter headings on sheets of note paper, allowing lots of room between headings. This provides a structure for lecture or reading notes. Of course, you can always modify notes by adding organizational categories. To repeat, the point is that you find some way of remaining an *active reader and notetaker.*

- **Use special features such as chapter summaries and study questions to focus your reading.** Read summaries and study questions *early* in your study of a chapter. They flag important concepts that you need to understand and that are likely to turn up on tests.

- **Bring your text to class regularly so that you can follow along with the instructor if he or she refers to it.**

- **Use self-sticking notes to flag *every* passage you find diffi-cult.** If a passage remains unclear after careful rereading, ask your instructor to go over it with you.

THE VIRTUES OF ANNOTATING AND OWNING YOUR OWN TEXT

Annotations are notes and comments written in the margins of a text by a reader. Though some people find it difficult to write in their books, annotating a text is a valuable study aid. Besides allowing you to annotate as you read, owning your own book allows you to study when it is most convenient. (Of course, you shouldn't annotate a text that you don't own.)

- **Annotate as you read; it prohibits passive reading and draws you into a meaningful conversation with other minds.** Annotating is a lot like a conversation conducted in writing. If you have ever looked through a book that's been annotated, you know how personal and interesting annotations can be. Looking through a book that has been annotated by someone else can be like observing another person's thinking process. The very activity of annotating a text requires you to respond to what you're reading: to inquire, praise, criticize, express delight or astonishment. When you review your annotated text, you'll probably refine your critique by reacting to your own annotations. Every time you review, rehash, react, and respond, you are refining and improving your understanding of what you read.

- **Make the text yours in a special way by annotating.** You create your own handy reference notes to use in class, to review for tests, or to research essays or term papers.

- **Be bold: Go beyond text highlighters and actually write in the margins.** Devise your own code, using *, !, ?, arrows, and so forth to indicate degrees of importance, agreement and disagreement, confusion, and so on.

- **Be critical, in a simple way.** Write *Yes,* or *No,* or even *B.S.* or *Wow!*—anything that works to get you involved in a dialogue with the text can help you better understand what you're reading.

- **If at all possible, buy your text with money you have earned or borrowed (and must repay yourself).** Spending your own money on the text is a way to reinforce your commitment to success to the class.

- **If necessary, find alternatives if you can't afford to purchase a text.** Most colleges have financial aid and short-term emergency loans available for students who cannot afford to buy necessary supplies. Taking the time and effort to secure aid or a loan is another way of reinforcing your commitment to success in a class.

- **Don't be overly concerned that annotating a text will diminish its resale value.** It probably will. But you have to decide how important succeeding in a particular class (and in college in general) is to you. If your only choice is between reselling your books and eating or dropping out of college, then perhaps you should not write in your books. But if you somehow can afford to rent videos, go to concerts, buy cokes and beer, order a pizza, buy CD's, and so forth, then you can afford to annotate your text—by giving up some of these luxuries for a while.

OUR BASIC READING STRATEGY SUMMARIZED

- **Skim the table of contents of each chapter to get an overview of what's in it.**

- **Read chapter summaries and review questions next.** (You might want to make a copy of the review questions to use as you study the chapter.)

- **Browse through the assigned sections and read whatever catches your eye, including margin quotes and boxed passages.**

- **Read the assignment once without worrying about taking notes or studying it carefully.** Remember to keep reading even if you think that you don't understand anything. You'll be surprised later to discover that you've picked up more than you realized.

- **Read the assignment a second time, more carefully.** Keep your self-sticking notes and copy of the review questions handy. Write out answers to study questions. Flag difficult passages.

- **Write the page numbers of passages that pertain to review questions next to the questions themselves.**

- **Begin making your own marginal notations at this stage.** Ask questions, jot down key ideas or terms that you'll want easy access to again. Make critical observations.

- **If necessary, reread the text a third time.**

- **Test your comprehension of key passages by restating them in your own words.** The best way to do this is by discussing the subject with another class member, friend, or relative. If that's not possible, pretend you are writing a letter to friend in which you want to explain a particular passage. If you cannot restate a passage in your own words, you don't understand it.

- **If necessary, reread the text a fourth time.**

WHAT TO DO IF NOTHING'S WORKING SO FAR

If you find it impossible to understand assigned readings after carefully following the steps discussed so far, you should consult your instructor and, probably, a counselor. You may discover that you need special classes in reading before you can succeed in philosophy. Take advantage of reading tests, reading labs, and related programs, if you need them.

Weak reading skills will not mysteriously disappear. Besides feeling frustrated and depressed because you cannot do as well as you want to, weak reading skills often result in low grades and serious long-term consequences.

Don't ignore a reading problem. Confront it as soon as you suspect its presence. Many times, special classes can quickly boost your performance. A wide variety of special programs are available for students with reading and learning difficulties.

CHAPTER 5

Critical Writing

The primary goals of critical writing are *argumentation, analysis*, and *evaluation*. Critical writing justifies a conclusion or interpretation by providing reasonable, relevant, and sufficient evidence to support it. The nature of the evidence depends on the specific way you choose to make your case and can include any combination of documented appeals to authoritative sources, language analysis, comparison and contrast, logical argumentation, and appeals to experience.

Creative writing, by contrast, values novelty, personal expression, imagination, and emotional impact, among other things. *Expository writing* focuses on presenting information in an organized, useful manner. Creative, expository, and critical writing often occur in the same text.

BASIC FEATURES OF GOOD CRITICAL WRITING

Most philosophy courses involve critical writing assignments of varying complexity and scope. They might include brief essay-type test questions, out-of-class essays, and longer term-paper assignments.

Certain common features apply to all good critical writing, regardless of length.

- **Good critical writing clearly identifies its main point (thesis) early.** Your reader should not have to read three or four pages or paragraphs to figure out what your main point is (or worse yet, have to *guess*). Your thesis (main point) should be clear in the opening paragraph.

- **Good critical writing avoids evasive, "weasel" claims.** The primary function of a weasel claim is to leave its author a way around criticism. Weasel claims make and evade a point at the same time. Consider this example: "It seems to me that Plato might have meant Z." Take a stand. Think. Did Plato mean Z or not?

- **Good critical writing documents its case so that readers can verify all important factual and scholarly claims for themselves.** Common forms of documentation include footnotes or endnotes.

- **Good critical writing avoids vague attributions.** Vague attributions, as the term implies, attribute positions to groups without offering documented details: "Virtually all Christians oppose abortions." "Most feminist philosophers favor abortion on demand."

  Vague attributions can be an indication of inferior research. They do not provide support for an argument because they don't tell the reader enough. Precisely which Christians or feminists hold these views, if any? Are they important ones or members of fringe groups? Furthermore, by not clearly identifying their sources, vague attributions don't tell us how current their content is. To the discerning reader, vague attributions suggest sloppy, uncritical reasoning.

  Vague attributions often signal bias and propaganda. Notice how Republican candidates vaguely refer to "the Democrats" and how Democratic candidates vaguely refer to "the Republicans." Different activist groups attribute offensive beliefs to atheists, secular humanists, liberals, fundamentalists, white people, and so forth. Without specifying precisely who said exactly what and in what context, claims supported by vague attributions function as propaganda, not evidence. Avoid sweeping, vague attributions. They never strengthen your case and almost always weaken it.

- **Good critical writing avoids vague appeals to "common sense" or "common knowledge":** "Everybody knows..."; "Decent people agree..." Such sweeping generalizations suffer from the same weaknesses as vague attributions. Furthermore, they are virtually meaningless, since they are either obviously false (as in the first example), or contain loaded, unclear terms that substitute for evidence (*decent* in the second example).

- **Good critical writing is organized.** It contains an opening statement of the thesis or topic, a main body, and a clearly identified summation-conclusion. Every paragraph is relevant. The text moves toward a clearly defined goal.

FOUR GREAT WRITING TIPS

1. **Start writing right away, and plan on revising your finished paper at least once.**

2. *Look at* **your finished paper.** Are the paragraphs one sentence long? one page long? If the paragraphs are uniformly long or short, the work may be poorly organized.

3. **Write the final versions of the introduction and the conclusion last.** Always match your introduction to your conclusion. A simple way to do this is to write only a tentative introduction to use as you develop your essay or paper. When you're finished with the body of the paper, word your conclusion in terms of what you've *actually shown*, and *then* write your final version of the introduction.

   If you've shown A, B, C, and D, your conclusion might include something like: "In this essay I began by showing A. Having done that, I explained how B and C follow from A. This led to my main point, D."

   After you've written the conclusion, write an introduction using key words and phrases from the conclusion. For example: "In this essay I begin by showing A. I next explain how B and C follow from A. This leads directly to my main point, D."

Framing your essay with a matching introduction and conclusion that *accurately describe* its content does three vital things: (1) It tells the reader what to expect. (2) It does what it promised to do. (3) It reminds the reader that it has done what it promised to do. Using key words and phrases in all three parts of the essay gives your work a polished coherence.

One of the saddest (yet avoidable) errors writers make is not matching the introduction and conclusion with each other and with the body of the paper. If you begin with the announcement that you will show A, B, C, and D and only show A, B, and C, you will have failed to substantiate your thesis. This is true even if D is a minor point.

Always double-check the introduction and conclusion *after* you've finished the final version of the body of the paper. **CAUTION:** This tip is not a substitute for good content. It will not obscure a weak effort.

4. **Let your paper get "cold" before you make your last editing pass.** Set your paper aside long enough to develop some critical distance before you make your last revision. You will spot major and minor problems much easier if you can read your own work with a fresh eye—and a sufficient lapse of time is the best way to do this.

HOW TO PICK A TOPIC

- **Start thinking about possible topics as soon as the assignment is made.** Flag passages in the text that might make good topics, even if you're not personally interested in them. At this stage, you want as many ideas as possible. Ideas breed ideas. Jot down thoughts, annoyances, or questions that provoke a response from you during lecture. Don't trust yourself to remember potential topics; write them down.

- **Think small.** One of the most common errors introductory philosophy students make in choosing a paper or essay topic is underestimating the amount of clarification and argumentation most critical writing requires. As a result, students sometimes pick huge topics that require writing a whole book. If you don't have much experience writing critically, follow this rule of thumb: *If you think a topic is too small, it's probably about right. It's better to have "too much" evidence than not enough.*

- **Word your topic precisely.** Vague topics tend to result in vague papers. Note the difference between these topics: "Existentialism" or "Sartre's Claim That We Choose the Adviser Most Likely to Tell Us What We Want to Hear." The second topic refers to a specific passage discussed in a textbook. The narrowness of the second topic is a virtue. It helps define and limit the writer's task. A general topic does not reflect an idea; it only indicates an area.

- **Don't take your topic personally.** You don't need to care about a subject to write well about it. Pick a topic that you can write well about in the amount of time you have. Be practical in your selection, considering what's going on in other courses you're taking, your job and family obligations, and your own actual work habits and abilities.

- **Forget about inspiration.** Don't fall into the trap of waiting for inspiration. Pick a topic as soon as you know the nature of the assignment. Waiting for inspiration may be a form of procrastination. Besides, inspiration may not come.

- **Unless you are an excellent critical writer, avoid defending your deepest personal beliefs.** For whatever reason, most of us are better at spotting weaknesses in ideas we dislike than we are at rationally supporting our own beliefs. A graded assignment in a philosophy class may not be the place to find out if you are an exception. Some of the poorest papers my colleagues and I receive are written in defense of the writer's most cherished beliefs. Their chief deficiency has been the substitution of heartfelt conviction and testimony for cogent argument and balanced documentation.

- **Remind yourself that there is no perfect topic.** Don't make more out of your topic selection than you have to. Your paper is not your last and only chance to say something on the subject. Your topic needs to be relevant to the course, adequate in scope yet not overwhelming, and researchable given your current resources. That's all.

A QUICK GUIDE TO GETTING BETTER GRADES ON WRITING ASSIGNMENTS

- **Pick a topic early** *and don't change it* **(unless you absolutely must).** Use the guidelines above to pick your topic. Then get right into it. Do any necessary research early. This will maximize the amount of time you have to process and refine your ideas.

- **If instructor approval is necessary, obtain it!** Students sometimes overlook or omit this step.

- **Just write!** As soon as you have done your initial preparation (which may range from studying a portion of your textbook to library research), write something. Write quickly, ignoring (for the moment) organization, grammar, and spelling. See where your mind wants to go. The very act of writing enhances the critical thinking process.

- **Form a semirough draft.** Now that you've written a first draft, you're ready to give it a more polished form. Shape paragraphs, move ideas around, elaborate, explain, clarify.

- **Define all key terms when you introduce them.** Be sure to specify exactly how you are using any key technical terms. *Do not use a conventional dictionary to define technical philosophical terms.* Conventional dictionaries only provide common, socially-correct usage. Doctors and lawyers use medical and legal dictionaries, and you should use a good philosophical dictionary, primary sources, references like the *Encyclopedia of Philosophy* (see bibliography) and your textbook to define key philosophical terms.

- **After you have written your first complete version, put it away and forget about it.** Let your work get cold. You'll need time to do this. That's why you picked a topic quickly and got to work early. Set the paper aside for a day or two at least; a week is better. This will help you acquire the critical distance you'll need to take an objective look at your work.

- **Critically revise.** Once you've established critical distance by setting your paper aside for a time, you're ready for careful revision. Read your paper as if you were grading it. Mark it up. As you read, ask yourself: "Is the thesis clearly stated? Does each step lead logically to what follows? Are important points supported with clearly stated reasons? Are terms used consistently? Are claims supported with documented sources, as needed? Does the paper make its case?" Improve the text as you answer these questions *with your thesis clearly in mind.*

- **If necessary, modify your original thesis.** Philosophical writers, once they have begun work on a topic, commonly discover that their original plan can be improved by selective modification. Perhaps too much is included, so some pruning is in order. Or perhaps what originally looked like a minor point has turned out to be crucial, so shifting and beefing up are in order. The point is, writing is not like captaining a ship. You're not honor bound to go down with a leaky vessel. Abandon a shaky topic if it can't be salvaged. Sometimes, there's no way to know that topic won't work for you until you have a go at it.

- **Don't be seduced by computerized spell-checkers and grammar-checkers.** Spell-checkers don't always contain technical philosophical terms. Spell-checking cannot catch the misuse of homonyms (words that sound alike) such as "two," "to," or "too." They don't catch correctly spelled but entirely inappropriate words. They don't catch omissions or redundancies. Different grammar-checkers have different protocols. None of them is entirely foolproof. You need to proofread your work even if you use these aides. To see why, study the following poem* that pops up on electronic bulletin boards:

I have a spelling checker,
It came with my PC;
It plainly marks four my revue
Mistakes I cannot sea.
I've run this pone threw it,
I'm sure your pleased to no,
It's letter perfect in its weigh,
My checker tolled me sew.
I only rote it one thyme,
Two let you here it rhyme,
Bee for I drank sum tee,
And inn my bed eye clime.

---

* Modified from Penney Harper, *National Notebook*, Spring 1993.

- **Don't confuse a good-looking, properly spelled, grammatically correct paper with a good paper.** Your professor has a right to expect a neat, grammatical paper. That's the minimum in philosophy classes, not the maximum. The mechanics of your paper should be "transparent," unnoticed by the reader. A mechanically correct paper allows its content to shine forth. Your philosophy professor may or may not mark grammatical errors, but he or she will certainly note them, and they will almost certainly damage the critical content of your writing.

- **Stop when you've made your point.** Don't pad your paper. Few philosophy instructors are impressed by sheer volume. You're probably better off saying less very precisely and coherently than saying more sloppily. As with all advice, make sure this suggestion applies to your circumstances. If your instructor places a premium on length, then pick your topic accordingly. You're still going to need to be clear and precise, however, no matter how long your paper is. Even if you have to write a long paper, don't pad it!

- **Document all sources.** *Plagiarism* occurs when you use someone else's exact words (or a close paraphrase) without giving them credit. Ironically, not citing sources almost always results in a poorer grade than crediting sources would have, because citing authorities and experts of established reputation adds their expertise and authority to your own excellent ideas. When you don't give credit to established experts, you deprive your paper of important support.

  Plagiarism in the form of *excessive paraphrasing* is usually easy to spot because the writing style of the text keeps shifting, and the content of some passages is too sophisticated for introductory-level work.

  If you find that you are going back and forth between reading and writing, always consulting your text, you are in danger of excessive paraphrasing. Your best safeguard is to use separate note cards to jot down all key quotations and brief summaries of key ideas. Organize your cards, and then write in your own words, inserting carefully selected and cited quotes.

  Any time you are using someone else's idea without significant modification, you need to document its originator. You have nothing to lose by citing good sources, and a great deal to lose by plagiarizing them, since penalties range from flunking an assignment to expulsion from college.

- **Follow instructions.** Let's admit it, many of the requirements instructors insist on are just their preferences. Who cares whether you use staples or paperclips, plastic covers or title sheets? *The person grading your work cares, that's who!* And that's a pretty good reason to follow instructions. It may not matter in the grand scheme of things whether you use footnotes, endnotes, or in-text citations. But if your instructor says endnotes, it matters to your grade. Use whatever style guide or manual your instructor requires. If none is specified, ask for guidance. Use the kind of paper, binder, and ink specified. Follow instructions regarding title pages and paperclips, margins, bibliographies, type size, spacing, and due dates. If your instructor has not specified these things, *ask.* Don't assume. Get clear information right away.

- **Use a good dictionary and approved style guide.** Simply assume that spelling and grammar count—don't embarrass yourself by asking. Consult your instructor regarding preferred style guidelines. (See the "Beginning Philosopher's Bibliography" for the names of some good style guides.)

- **Type your work.** Other things being equal, neatly typed assignments get higher grades than handwritten ones. Take advantage of this fact. (But neat garbage is still garbage, and neatly typed garbage is a waste of everybody's time.)

- **Stick to the length specified.** Unless explicitly told otherwise, use conventional margins, double-space, and use 10- or 12-point font if you have a word processor. Play fair. Don't try to pad a thin paper with huge printing and exaggerated margins, and don't exceed length requirements with small print, small margins, and space-and-a-half printing. To be safe, try to get a specified word-count rather than page length.

- **Proofread your final draft.** It is much better to make neat corrections by hand than to ignore typos, spelling errors, bad grammar, and gross inconsistencies. If you have more than two or three corrections on a page, retype it. *This is another reason to allow plenty* *of time for the entire writing process, from topic selection to typing or print-ing the final version.*

- **Keep at least one copy of your paper in a safe place.** Your instructor is not the one who will suffer if your paper is lost or damaged.

- **Turn in the original or a high-quality photocopy, not a smudged, black-edged, or faint photocopy.**

- **Use a good ribbon or printer, and do not use onionskin, easy-erase, or colored paper.**

- **Plan ahead to get to school early on the due date.** Some in-structors penalize late papers. Allow for possible transportation problems and other contingencies.

- **If you need special consideration, talk to your instructor as soon as you are aware of special needs.** Don't be embarrassed to request special consideration if you really need it. On the other hand, don't think that just being busy or apprehensive about writ-ing a paper is a special need. Most students are very busy, and at least moderately nervous, about turning in written work.

- **Always study your graded paper.** Try to understand why your instructor gave you that grade. If you need more explanation than is provided with the graded paper, politely request it.

- **Cool off before you decide you were cheated on your grade.** If you feel that your grade is inaccurate, *after setting the paper aside for a few days and carefully rereading it,* courteously request a rereading by your instructor.

- **If your instructor does not return graded papers, make an appointment to review and discuss your paper during office hours.** If you plan to discuss your paper with the instructor, give him or her time to review it before the discussion.

FOUR WRITING SAMPLES FOR YOU TO GRADE

Next to writing experience, perhaps the best way to improve your critical writing is by reading other people's critical writing. In some writing courses, students exchange essays and rough drafts of papers for the purpose of offering positive criticism. They help one another identify strengths and weaknesses, and get a better idea of how good writing differs from poor writing.

The following essays were written by students in an introduction to philosophy course. The essays were written in class as part of an announced closed-book test. Two weeks before the test, the instructor distributed a list of questions from which the test question would be selected. The questions all referred to specific topics covered in Chapter 18 of the textbook *Archetypes of Wisdom: An Introduction to Philosophy, Second Edition*. Sartre's claim that "existence precedes essence" was discussed at length in class, as well. The students were asked: "What did Sartre mean by the phrase *existence precedes essence*? Why is the issue important? Do you agree with Sartre? Explain."

As you read each of the unedited essays, use the following questions as guidelines for your evaluation. See whether you think the essays clearly and directly answer the question.

- Would an intelligent reader who is unfamiliar with Sartre's idea get a clear introduction to its meaning from the essay?

- Does the essay give evidence of familiarity with the assigned readings? For instance, does it use specific examples or concepts from the text?

- Are the sentences grammatically correct and is the essay well organized (given the time constraints of an in-class essay)?

- On the basis of your answers to these questions, what grade would you give each essay? Why?

Note: It's a good idea to read all four essays before assigning grades to any of them.

Sample Essay Question:
What did Sartre mean by the phrase "existence precedes essence"?
Why is the issue important? Do you agree with Sartre? Explain.

Sample Essay 1

He means that you first must be a human on this earth before you have
an essence. This is important because if you are not in existence then how
can there be essence. Existence is very important. I agree with this because I also feel that there must be existence before essence. This is important for humans as well as others. Sartre had his own ways and so do
many others, of everything.

Sample Essay 2

Sartre meant that you as a person are not born a certain way. Nobody is
born a coward or is born a bad person. The person has control over their
own actions and if they <u>choose</u> to be brave they will do brave things just
as if they only committed cowardly acts they would be cowards but by
choice. This is important because if it were true then a person could not
excuse behavior such as robbery or murder just because they had a bad
childhood or they were in a violent neighborhood and couldn't help it. I
agree with Sartre. To me you always have a choice and I think that making excuses like the ones above are a "copout". Even if you decide not to
choose between two evils you still have made a choice. There is always a
choice and we have free will.

Sample Essay 3

Existence precedes essence means that "you are fundamentally what you do." You are your actions. There is no "essence" that you are born with. Your actions shape you & make you what you are. You must decide upon your actions & be responsible for them. You are free to choose but must face the consequences they bring. I agree with Sartre.

Sample Essay 4

What Sartre meant by existence precedes essence is that our actions and choices develop our values. In a simpler manner, what we do is what we are. People are not born with certain values. They make choices and act in the value spectrum they choose.

Sartre said "Consciousness has incalculable consequences." He did not like the excuse that I can do something bad because not everybody does it. He said to choose with our eyes open and with responsibility. Sartre's idea was in contrast to Kant's philosophy of motives. Sartre said we are condemned to be free because there is no God. So everything is permitted.

I agree sort of. I do not agree about God. I believe in God. But I do think what we do is more important than what we think. I do not like excuses. But sometimes I think people can't help what they do. So I guess I think existence precedes essence most of the time. But some people, babies and brain damaged people, are not free. So how can they be condemned to be free?

A LAST LOOK AT THE FOUR SAMPLE ESSAYS

You're probably wondering what grades the four sample essays actually got.

- **Sample Essay 1 received an F.** It is much too general, and most of what it does say is confusing. *Nothing* in the essay indicates familiarity with the assigned readings. The essay is too short and repeats what little it does say. The sentence "I agree with this because I also feel that there must be existence before essence" is a form of a fallacy known as *begging the question*. Begging the question occurs when an argument uses some form of its conclusion as evidence for that very conclusion. In this case, the author of the essay has really said nothing more than "I agree with Sartre because I agree with him."

- **Sample Essay 2 received a B+.** By opening with the example of being born a coward, the author of Sample Essay 2 signals the reader that he or she is familiar with the assignment. The author then proceeds to develop the idea, using the concepts of choice and excuse making. This at least implies recognition of the importance of responsibility to Sartre. The closing reference to free will indicates awareness of another important, related issue. Compare this essay's fuller statement to the begged question which concludes Sample Essay 1: "I agree with Sartre. To me you always have a choice and I think that making excuses like the ones above are a 'copout.' Even if you decide not to choose between two evils you still have made a choice. There is always a choice and we have free will."

- **Sample Essay 3 received a C–.** This essay is clear, and what it does say is *generally correct*. But it is also repetitive. Worse, the essay does not make it clear that the author studied the assigned reading. That's a big problem with "generally o.k." essays. Furthermore, the writer merely states "I agree with Sartre," without offering any explanation, as is called for in the instructions. A cynical reader could interpret this essay as being *evasive*. That is, the lack of specific examples from the assigned readings, combined with the repetition, could be interpreted as evidence of failure to read the assignment thoroughly, or at all. A more charitable reader might assume that the writer knew more than he or she said, and attribute the essay's weaknesses to lack of writing experience. The essay is weak because it is ambiguous and vague.

- **Sample Essay 4 received an A–.** This essay contains multiple references to the assigned readings, making it very clear that its author has studied them. Although overall the essay is clear, the last two sentences in the first paragraph are not: "People are not born with certain values. They make choices and act in the value spectrum they choose." Whatever this writer meant needed clarification. The statement "Sartre said 'Consciousness has incalculable consequences' " is not entirely correct. Sartre did not *say* that in so many words. The student is confusing a characterization of Sartre's ideas by the textbook's author with Sartre's own words. But this kind of "error" on an in-class, closed-book test is trivial. The essay makes it clear that this student did the assignment, even going so far as to memorize what he or she recognized as an important point. Finally, compare this writer's explanation of why he or she agrees with Sartre with the closing remarks in the other three essays. This writer's explanation is the most sophisticated of the four because it is a *qualified* agreement, accepting some of Sartre's ideas, but not all of them—and offering examples to support the writer's point of view: "I agree sort of. I do not agree about God. I believe in God. But I do think what we do is more important than what we think. I do not like excuses. But sometimes I think people can't help what they do. So I guess I think existence precedes essence most of the time. But some people, babies and brain damaged people, are not free. So how can they be condemned to be free?"

How did your grades compare with each essay's actual grades?

CHARACTERISTICS OF GOOD AND BAD ESSAYS

Many students think that essay assignments and tests are subjective in the sense that they have no one right answer. Perhaps you've had the common experience of being absolutely convinced that you were cheated on an essay assignment because you wrote "the same thing" as your friend who got a better grade. This may be correct in some cases, but remember that no matter how similar two essays are, they are not exactly the same. Grades can be affected by the order in which topics are covered, word choice, organization (paragraphing), sentence structure, nature and number of examples, degree of specificity, and so forth. Your essay may be very similar to your friend's, but your professor is probably responding to the *whole essay effect*, as well as to individual aspects that your essay may share with your friend's.

Does this mean that essay grades are subjective in the sense of being capricious or arbitrarily relative? In fact, there is a high degree of consistency among grading standards of experienced professors. Professor W may be slightly tougher than Professor Y, so that a B+ from Professor W is roughly equivalent to an A from Professor Y, but the *relative rankings* of their grades will tend to conform. That means that it is highly unlikely that an essay that gets an A from Professor Y would get a D or an F from Professor W.

In doing the research for this book, I have identified certain common characteristics that affect the way many professors grade essays. Knowing what these are can help you write better essays and papers (since papers and essays share many fundamental features). Here's what I found, which, incidentally, reaffirmed my own grading practices.

- **Spelling and grammar almost always matter.** Having a grammatically correct essay cannot substitute for not knowing the material, but poor grammar and spelling detract from even the best ideas.

- **Length matters, but not in a simplistic way.** Essays that call for explanation, elaboration, or critical evaluation must be long enough to cover everything asked for. Past that point, however, length is not a reliable indicator of quality. A lot of irrelevant, unclear, or incorrect material only underscores lack of preparation. Good essays avoid padding.

- **Good essays answer the question as it is asked.** This is just another form of following instructions, which is always fundamental. Writing brilliantly about something else, even something closely related to the assignment, is not a substitute for showing your professor that you understand the specific material he or she wants to test you on.

- **Good essays offer reasonable, relevant, sufficient evidence to support their claims.** Poor essays tend to settle for merely making assertions or offering vague or sweeping statements as support.

- **Good essays are specific.** Good essays use precise, correct terms from assigned readings. Good essays refer to individuals by name on a regular basis. Poor essays use *he, she,* or *they* too often.

- **Good essays make it very clear that their writers are familiar with *both* assigned readings *and* lectures.** This is another way of being specific, rather than general and vague.

- **Good essays reflect organized thought.** Good take-home essays are well structured and organized. Sufficiently well organized in-class essays indicate careful studying and planning. Jumbled, chaotic take-home essays imply lack of preparation and effort. Jumbled, chaotic in-class essays are more difficult to interpret, but assuming that you have the prerequisite language skills for a philosophy class, poorly organized work suggests lack of preparation.

- **Excellent essays provide unique examples and explanations.** Excellent essays reflect a solid grasp of the material, but in their own unique voice. They do not just repeat examples and explanations from the text and lectures.

- **Excellent essays draw conclusions and make inferences that go beyond class material.** These can be in the form of questions, criticisms, identification of inconsistencies, and so forth.

- **Essays decline in quality with each of the following weaknesses:**

  √ **Misspelled names and key terms:** This implies that the writer has not read the material at all or has not studied it carefully. At the very least, you should identify all key figures and technical terms and memorize their correct spellings.

  √ **Factual errors:** These include attributing ideas to the wrong philosopher, or distorting a philosopher's views.

√ **Irrelevant material:** Weak essays rely on irrelevant personal comments and anecdotes ("I had a lot of trouble picking a topic. At first I was going to write about Plato...") or distracting analyses of concepts that do not directly answer the question as it is framed.

√ **Unexplained or unsupported key assertions:** The last sentence in Sample Essay 3 is a classic example of this error. Repeating the same point in different words is a common variant of this mistake, since merely asserting something more than once does not suddenly become evidence for its truth.

√ **Mere listing of lots of ideas:** Students express considerable frustration when they believe that they have "included everything you said was important." Certainly that's a necessary first step in writing a good analytic or critical essay. But a *critical essay* is different from a *summary* or *report*. A list or summary is not a substitute for a cogent analysis.

A SIMPLIFIED STYLE GUIDE FOR EXCELLENT PAPERS

Here's a simple, generic style guide that should be sufficient for most introductory-level philosophy papers and essays. Before you use it, however, check with your instructor.

- **Handwritten papers:** Standard size (8 1/2 x 11 inches), wide-lined notebook paper. Use black or dark blue ink. Write on one side of the page. Do not use sheets torn out of a spiral-bound notebook.

- **Typed papers:** Standard size (8 1/2 x 11 inches), heavy paper (not onionskin and not easy-erase paper—it smudges). Good, black ribbon or printer with plenty of ink or toner. Double-space. Use only one side of the page. Do not use fancy type.

- **Word processors:** Same as typed plus: 10- or 12-point font. Avoid excessive use of graphics and fancy print styles. Concentrate on content. Print copy should be set to highest quality (not draft mode).

- **Margins:** One and one-half inch left and top; one inch right and bottom. (Ruled, red line for margins on lined notebook paper.)

- **Indenting:** Indent the first line of all paragraphs five spaces or about one-half inch.

- **Paragraphs:** Double space as usual between paragraphs—do not leave extra space.

- **Quotations:** If a quote runs more than three lines, indent the entire quote, and cite your source. If it runs less than three lines, imbed it in the text (don't forget quotation marks), and cite your source.

- **Page numbers:** Number every page except the title page in the upper right-hand corner. Use Arabic numerals (1, 2, 3, etc.).

- **Fasteners:** Unless your instructor tells you otherwise, staple your paper together in the upper left-hand corner. Do not use binders or covers; do not use paper clips; never, ever use the old "pinch, tear, and fold" method—unless specifically instructed to do so.

- **Supplies: Do not expect your instructor, or the college, to provide you with staples, paper clips, binders, and such:** It is your responsibility to have your paper completely finished and ready to hand in by the date and time your instructor specifies.

- **Computer Access: If you are planning to use the college's computer lab to write your paper, check out lab schedules and computer availability right away:** If necessary, sign up for ample computer time. Budget time for emergencies and down time.

- **Typists: If you are hiring a typist, allow plenty of time to proofread and, if necessary, retype the final draft:** Be very clear with the typist regarding how much time he or she will need, and so forth. Begin lining up a good typist early, and stay in touch once you find one. *Remember that no matter who helps you prepare your paper, you are the one responsible for fulfilling all requirements— and you're the one getting graded.*

• **A sample title page:**

TITLE   (all caps)

by

Ima Student

Date: September 1, 1995

Class: Philosophy 1A   Instructor: Ms. Gaea

- **Citations:** Number *all* direct quotes and paraphrases of others' ideas at the end of the quote or the last sentence of the paraphrase. Number footnotes/endnotes consecutively throughout the paper.

- **Footnotes and endnotes:** Document quotations and paraphrases with sequentially numbered references. You may cite your references at the bottom of each page (footnotes) or on a page immediately following the body of your paper (endnotes). Endnotes are preferable if you don't have a powerful word processor. Footnotes involve the complication of figuring out when to end the main text on each page to allow exactly enough space for the footnotes.

  If you use endnotes, title the page immediately following your conclusion ENDNOTES. Number all endnote pages. You won't need a bibliography if you cite all of your sources in the endnotes.

- **Basic citation forms: <u>Underline</u> or *italicize* the titles of books and journals. Put magazine and journal article titles in quotation marks.** If you are using a typewriter that does not have an *italics* mode or are handwriting your paper, underline all titles. If you are using a sophisticated printer and word processor, you can either <u>underline</u> or *italicize* titles; just be consistent.

  Books: The first time you list a book in your endnotes, follow this form (paying special attention to punctuation):

  Footnote #. Author name, <u>Title</u> (City of publisher: Publisher), Date, page #.

  Identify translators or editors after the title. Here are some book citation examples:

  3. Douglas Soccio, <u>Archetypes of Wisdom: An Introduction to Philosophy</u>, Second Edition (Belmont, Calif.: Wadsworth Publishing Company), 1995, pp. 59–63.

  4. Karl Jaspers, <u>Socrates, Buddha, Confucius, Jesus: The Paradigmatic Individuals,</u> ed. Hannah Arendt, trans. Ralph Manheim (New York: Harcourt Brace Jovanovich), 1962, p. 87.

  5. Daniel Kolak and Raymond Martin, <u>The Experience of Philosophy</u> (Belmont, Calif.: Wadsworth Publishing Company), 1990, p. 200.

For subsequent citations from a source follow this simple form (paying special attention to punctuation): Title, p. #. Examples:

13. <u>Archetypes of Wisdom: An Introduction to Philosophy</u>, p. 112.

14. <u>The Experience of Philosophy</u>, p. 67.

16. <u>Socrates, Buddha, Confucius, Jesus: The Paradigmatic Individuals</u>, p. 80.

When you cite the same source more than once in an uninterrupted sequence, use: <u>Ibid</u>. If the page numbers change, use: <u>Ibid</u>., p. #. Examples:

18. <u>The Experience of Philosophy</u>, p. 12.

19. <u>Ibid</u>.

20. <u>Ibid</u>., p. 18.

Articles: Follow this format: Author, "Article Title." <u>Magazine or Journal Title</u>, volume number, date, first page number. Here are some examples:

33. Joelson, J. R., "English: The Language of Liberty." <u>The Humanist</u>, July/Aug. 1989, p. 35.

34. Gilmar, Sybil T., "Language Foreign to U. S. School," Editorial. <u>Philadelphia Inquirer</u>, April 25, 1990, p. A17.

35. Maloconico, Joseph, "New Influx of Immigrants." <u>New Jersey News-Tribune</u>, March 1991, p. A1.

36. Shumway, Norman D., "Make English the Official Language," Letter. <u>Chicago Tribune</u>, August 30, 1992, sec. 4, p. 2.

37. "Lessons from the U. S. Army." <u>Fortune</u>, March 22, 1993, p. 68.

Citation 37 is for an anonymous article, so no author is listed.

CAUTION: This is a *simplified* style guide. Be sure your instructor approves of its use.

A HANDY CHECKLIST FOR BETTER CRITICAL WRITING

Review these questions before you begin to write and then again as you proofread and revise your work.

_____ Is the first paragraph so clear that an intelligent reader who is not familiar with your topic will understand exactly what that topic is?

_____ Is the first paragraph so clear that any intelligent reader will understand exactly what your strategy for dealing with the topic is?

_____ Are all sentences grammatically correct?

_____ Are all technical terms spelled correctly?

_____ Is your essay or paper well organized?

_____ Does your essay or paper use specific examples and language that show that you are familiar with the assigned readings and any other important material?

_____ Does your essay or paper end with a clear and obvious summation and conclusion, keyed precisely and directly to what you say in the body of the text?

_____ Have you carefully proofread the final version of your essay or paper?

PART THREE

Student Wisdom

You already possess most of the skills and abilities necessary to succeed in college: Have you noticed how much time fans put into reading about their interests? How much time and energy people put into tinkering on their cars or decorating their homes or playing basketball? How much money is spent on hobbies? How much sweat, work, energy, and sacrifice go into leisure activities? Have you noticed how easy it is to remember the date and starting time of the big game or concert—even if it's weeks away?

These are the very same habits and abilities that make successful students. The difference between spending two hours a night reading sports magazines and two hours studying philosophy is due as much to lack of interest and motivation as it is to lack of ability.

Part Three is a summary of lots of good advice, what I think of as *student wisdom*. Some of it will be new to you, but much of will not. Combining new advice with reminders of what you already know about school success can strengthen your commitment to your education, and inspire you when the going gets rough.

Chapter 6 is full of excellent time-saving and motivational tidbits. Chapter 7 contains time-tested guidelines for having rich, rewarding relationships with your professors. Chapter 8 is a distillation of expert tips on taking tests. The "Bibliography for Beginning Philosophers" lists a variety of effective manuals and reference materials that can smooth your educational journey.

CHAPTER 6

Basic Motivation And Strategy For Getting The Most Out Of College

Before reading the rest of this chapter, fill in the form on the next page. Write all the reasons you have for going to college. List your *real* reasons, not your public ones. If you are going to college because you need a degree to get a certain kind of job, say so. If you're going to college to put off getting a "real job," say so. Don't feel pressured to pretend that you want to broaden yourself if you're really in college because you don't know what else to do at this stage of your life. List as many reasons as you have. Any reason for going to college can be a good reason, if you learn something important while you're there.

My Reasons For Going To College

_____

_____

_____

_____

_____

_____

_____

_____

_____

_____

_____

_____

_____

_____

_____

_____

_____

_____

_____

_____

_____

_____

_____

_____

_____

Take a moment to review your list. If you're like most students, you'll have a variety of reasons for being in college, including a general desire to learn, a desire for the social prestige attached to being a college graduate, and the hope that a degree will lead to a financially comfortable and personally rewarding career.

Whatever your current reasons, note that given your present circumstances, *you have decided that going to college is better than all of the alternatives.* When you get discouraged, remind yourself that you are where you have decided it's best to be at the moment.

Keep your list handy, and read it when you need a boost: before tests, during difficult projects, when you're feeling sorry for yourself because you need to study but want to party or have more time for your family, or whenever you wonder "Why am I doing this?" Note that these are *your* reasons. Add to them as you discover additional ones for going to college.

Regularly reassess your goals. An academic or vocational degree requires a significant investment of time, effort, and money. Failure to identify your own clear reasons for going to college can result in wasting all three.

At the same time, part of the educational process is ongoing self-discovery that often results in new goals, so don't be discouraged if your plans change two or three times during your college career. The crucial thing is to be as clear as you can about *your real* goals. No one else's opinions about college can give you the energy and commitment required for college success.

Here's a bit of advice that may anger some of the people in your life: *It's all right if this is not the time for you be in college.* You're the only one who can get deep enough into your motives to know what's right for you now. If you are not ready to concentrate and sacrifice, or if you have too many complications in your personal life, you may be wise to wait before going on with your education. You do not want to use up limited financial aid while you're distracted or poorly motivated. And you don't want a weak transcript, since a weak transcript won't help you get a job, and can make it difficult (or impossible) to go on with your education in the future.

On the other hand (philosophers always have another hand to cloud the issue), be very sure that you have exhausted all your resources before deciding to quit college. If you're worried about money or working too much, talk to a good financial aid adviser. You might be eligible for a scholarship you've never heard of, or a loan, or additional work study. Find out what opportunities your college offers for child care, if that's a concern. Make sure you don't just need more rest, or glasses, or to take one fewer course per term. Don't let one instructor or course stop you. Check on evening classes at your own college and other nearby colleges if the only instructor for a required course is offensive to you.

SET REALISTIC GOALS

- **Identify *your* strengths and weaknesses as objectively as possible.** You can do this informally or go to the college counseling center for career interest and skills testing.

- **Respect *your* interests.** If you've always hated school, don't choose a major that requires years of it. If you've never liked children, don't plan to become a teacher just because that job market is good.

- **Respect *your* talents.** Take advantage of your natural abilities. If you're a natural socializer and conversationalist who's always been able to make feel people comfortable and who can relate to practically anybody, you'll probably be happier as a teacher or social worker than as a research chemist or forest ranger.

  Be creative as you explore your options. A natural socializer might become a happy, first-rate hotel manager or cruise-ship entertainment director instead of a teacher or social worker. On the other hand, maybe you've always been good with details, even as a child. You like order and instinctively arrange things logically. Academic and career areas that are subject to creative disarray and require subjective interpretation may not be your best choice. Drama, literature, and working with small children may frustrate you, but accounting, office management, or computer processing may not.

- **When you have no clear direction, experiment.** Take any classes that interest you for two or three terms. See if they show a pattern. If they do, fashion your newly identified interests into a workable major. If they don't, consider taking a break from college.

- **Take advantage of your school's career center.** There are probably many career options that you are not aware of. Get some expert help in identifying them.

- **Base your immediate goals on your current life circumstances.** Realistically consider family obligations, job requirements, the demands of specific courses, transportation needs (and time), and so forth as you plan your educational strategy.

- **Continually monitor your *progress* and your *satisfaction*.** Modify your goals accordingly.

- **Don't try to take on too much at once.** Superman and Superwoman are fictional characters; they don't exist in real life. You may discover that your state of mind and performance significantly improve by taking one less class a term, or working five fewer hours a week. While a certain amount of tension can be good for you, too much can result in overload and inefficiency.

- **Remember that you can always change your mind.**

TIME MANAGEMENT

By the end of the first week of the term, you should have a general idea of how much time you'll need for each of your classes. Counselors usually suggest allowing *three hours of study for every one hour of class.* Plan a tentative study schedule, allowing time for daily assignments, major projects, and test preparation. You can modify this schedule as experience warrants. Be sure to include regular leisure activity, exercise, and rest. Try to allow some leeway for unexpected emergencies, improvised social activities, and other unforeseeable needs. *Academic counselors report that failure to establish and stick to a regular study schedule is the most common characteristic shared by students with poor grades or who ultimately drop out of college.*

Use the simple form on the next page to get an idea of the kind of commitment you will need to make to succeed in college.

Time Budget
(There are 168 hours in a week)

Total hours spent on campus per week (time in class, at team practices and games, student government, in the library, labs)	_____
3 hours × _____ **units for out-of-class study**	_____
Total hours worked per week	_____
_____ **hours for sleep** × **7 nights**	_____
Total hours per week for necessities (cooking, eating, shopping, bathing, laundry, yardwork, etc.)	_____
Total hours per week for family duties (driving children to various activities, helping with homework, helping other relatives, attending church, and so forth)	_____
Total hours per week for exercise	_____
Total commuting hours per week	_____
TOTAL OBLIGATED HOURS PER WEEK	_____
168 hours in a week	**168**
minus total obligated hours	=_____
equals FREE TIME PER WEEK	_____

ACCEPT WHAT YOU CAN'T CHANGE

The wise Hasidic Rabbi Zusya once said, "When I get to heaven, they will not ask me, Why were you not Moses?, they will ask me, Why were you not Zusya?"

It can be frustrating when other people get better grades than you do without studying as much as you do. But the harsh fact is that the only value someone else's grades and study habits can have for you is informational. If you can learn something from them that will improve your comprehension, skills, and performance, good. If not, your best bet is to ignore the seeming injustice of it all, and study as much as *you* need to.

It can be annoying when the instructor gives multiple-choice tests and you excel at essays (or vice-versa). It's doubly disturbing when the test questions are trivial or seem irrelevant. But once you discover the instructor's style of testing, your best bet is to accommodate yourself to it. You may wish to respectfully offer reasonable alternatives, but you must ultimately deal with the less-than-perfect tests you are given.

This kind of accommodation is not the same thing as selling out. It is grounded in academic realty: As a rule, students don't get to write or individualize their tests and assignments. Act the role of the wise student. Don't get trapped in the role of resentful would-be-instructor.

Distinguish between accommodating yourself to the unavoidable inequities of academic life and serious unethical inequalities. Not all compromises involve your very essence.

CHANGE WHAT YOU CAN

Respectfully exert what influence you can to improve your courses, but learn when to cease in these efforts and get on with doing as well as you can, given the particular demands of the course.

- **Don't punish yourself.** If a course is truly beyond your current abilities or the instructor is demeaning, unprofessional, unprepared, and so forth, get out.

- **Don't shortchange yourself.** If you've been attending class and keeping up with assignments, trust your gut reactions. Ask the questions that occur to you during lecture, and make thoughtful comments. Give yourself credit for being able to identify issues that need clarification. Even if your instructor modifies or corrects what you say, you will have learned something, reinforced your self-respect, and polished your skills at rational discourse. How can you lose with that combination?

- **In any area where you are experiencing frustration and difficulty, consider a fresh approach.** If you've been studying philosophy after dinner, try studying at some other time. Try sitting in a different seat. Change the way you take notes. The point is, if things aren't working well, don't be too quick to dismiss alternatives. Something that seems silly or unpromising may surprise you. (Of course if the new approach only makes things worse, stop using it.) I know this sounds obvious and too simple, but you'd be surprised at how many students refuse to try new approaches because they prejudge them as unhelpful.

AVOID FALSE COMPARISONS

You may know the folk legend of John Henry. John Henry worked on the railroad, using two 9-pound hammers to drive the steel spikes that hold the rails to the ties. Shortly after the invention of the steam engine, the railroads began to replace steel drivers with steam-powered machines that would ultimately put hundreds of men out of work. According to the legend, John Henry challenged one of the new machines to a spike-driving contest and "won." Swinging a hammer in each hand, the powerful John Henry drove more spikes than the machine. But he was so exhausted from the effort that he "laid down his hammer and he died."

Many people see the story of John Henry in terms of one man's courage in the fight against the replacement of human beings by machines. There's another lesson, too. We can kill ourselves trying to be what we're not. John Henry was not a machine. He could not be expected to do a machine's work. No amount of desire, courage, or righteousness could change the harsh reality of John Henry's relation to the machine.

You may have untapped potential and room to grow, but you are a unique individual. You cannot become the student sitting next to you, your mother, pal, teacher, or fictionalized ideal. Learn from others, but don't condemn yourself for not being them. And don't exhaust yourself trying to be someone you're not.

If you're interested in the issue of "becoming yourself," you can read more about it in Chapter 7, "The Naturalist: Aristotle," in *Archetypes of Wisdom, Second Edition*. The following passage from the Trappist monk and philosopher Thomas Merton (1915–1968) is from that chapter. Reread it when you're criticizing yourself for not being someone else:

> Many [people] ... never become the [person] who is called for by all the circumstances of their individual lives. They waste their years in vain efforts to be some other [person].... For many absurd reasons, they are convinced that they are obliged to become somebody else.... They wear out their minds and bodies in a hopeless endeavor to have somebody else's experiences or write somebody else's poems or express somebody else's spirituality.

- **Remember that sometimes it takes courage to do something, and sometimes it takes courage to quit (especially if others will be disappointed).** If John Henry had paid closer attention to himself, he would have known that he was taxing his heart beyond its endurance. Even though he "won" the challenge, he lost in the long run. It's sometimes better to quit early than to quit late. (But be sure that you're quitting for good reasons, and not just to avoid studying hard.)

- **Resist comparisons that lead to resentment.** We all know that life is not particularly fair. Resentment won't improve your grades, and it can pollute your emotions in a way that actually interferes with good study habits.

- **March to your own beat.** If other people pressure you to proceed at a pace that's inappropriate for you, or if they make fun of you for lacking certain skills, remind yourself that they will not suffer if you have to drop out of college, and they won't pay your student loans if you can't keep up. In other words, *you are the one who will pay the price if you fail to meet **their** expectations.* Your friends and family shouldn't expect you to make their credit card payments—and they shouldn't expect you to make their "life payments." If they do expect you to, resist in the best way you can.

WHAT IT REALLY COSTS TO GO TO COLLEGE

Don't forget that going to college is your choice. Resist thinking that you "have" to do your assignments. The reality is that you are being given the *privilege* of doing your assignments. No fixed law of nature, morality, or society forces you to go to college or take a philosophy course. Going to college and taking philosophy are the clearly marked price tags for something of greater value: a good education and future successes and opportunities.

- **Remind yourself that the full price of your education includes more than the monetary cost of fees and supplies.** You must pay with time, effort, and a temporarily modified social life. You'll get the best education by paying full price. Trying to "have it all" commonly results in frustration, anxiety, fatigue, and possible failure.

- **Regularly tell yourself that being a college student is only a temporary condition.** College may seem to go on forever, but it doesn't. You will have a "real life" someday. (And if you're like many of us, you'll look back on your years in college as "the good old days.")

- **Realize that the typical 3-unit semester course consists of fewer than 48 hours spent in class.** That's only 2 days. If you study 3 hours for every class-hour, you'll add only 6 days, bringing the total to a week and 1 day. Generously allowing another 2 full weeks for total time spent on term papers and so forth, one 3-unit class involves a total of 3 weeks and 1 day. And for those students who do not study 3 hours for every hour spent in class, a 3-unit class takes even less time.

- **Think of going to college as your primary job.** Job requirements include: regular attendance; doing assignments; spending money on supplies instead of pizza and beer; listening to ideas you don't like or have no personal interest in; taking good notes; paying attention; and study, study, study.

- **When you get frustrated and resent paying the price, review this lesson from the *Enchiridion* of the Stoic sage Epictetus (c. 50–130):**

  You will be unjust then and insatiable, if you do not part with the price, in return for which ... things are sold, and if you wish to obtain them for nothing. Well, what is the price of lettuces?

An obulus perhaps. If then a man gives up the obulus and receives the lettuces, and if you do not give up the obulus and do
not receive the lettuces, do not suppose that you receive less
than he who has got the lettuces; for as he has the lettuces, so
you have the obulus which you did not give ...

If another student gives up the obulus by devoting time to philosophy, and by studying harder and more frequently than you do, don't
compound your problems by resenting her better grade. She has a
good grade in philosophy; you have your obulus (time used for other
things).

Perhaps you're thinking, "But it's not that simple. I have a job and
family—the other student doesn't. It's easy for her to study. I'd like
to see what kind of grades she gets in my circumstances." Put that
curiosity to rest, and review the preceding section on false comparisons. Remind yourself that you will never be able to see what kind
of grades another student would get in your circumstances because
you are an essential component of what makes your circumstances
your circumstances.

And whether or not life is fair is a deep philosophical problem that
you have a lifetime to wrestle with. Right now, you need to maximize your actual circumstances. Think carefully about the "obuluses"
in your life. Are you perhaps trying to "clip the coin a trifle" and not
pay the full price? If so, you need to decide whether the quality of
your education (and all that is connected with it) warrants more effort and sacrifice while you're in college. If you are truly out of resources and cannot pay the price, then you need to deal with that.

It's probably not fair that some people have it easier than others.
But if life is not fair, then there's no reason to waste time harping on
it or foolishly waiting for some one or some thing to make it fair.
Maybe one shouldn't charge a whole obulus for a lettuce, but until
you are in a position to open a market or grow your own lettuce,
about all you can do is decide to keep the obulus *or* acquire the lettuce.

As long as you're paying for a college education—and every student pays something—you might as well pay what it costs to get a
good one.

IT'S WORTH THE EFFORT

- **The typical 3-unit semester course meets for less than 48 hours.** That's right: less than 2 days of class time. If you take 4 courses, that's 8 days per semester, or 16 per year (20 days per year if you take 5 courses). If you graduate from a 2-year program, you may be in class for *35–40 days*. You can double that for the typical bachelor's degree to *70–80 days*. (Typically, students who take 5 or 6 years to get their bachelor's degrees spend additional hours at work, not in class, so the total stays the same.) Even adding the hours needed for studying, and the cost of tuition, and supplies, and room and board, college is a bargain.

- **Lack of a college degree is a burden in today's economy, no matter what else affects your chances for a satisfying job.** Most students go to college in the hopes that having a college degree will lead to a high-paying, prestigious job. Unfortunately, things aren't that simple. As more and more people graduate from college, the marketplace significance of having a college education diminishes. Ironically, that means that the significance of *not* having a college education *increases*. As a college degree becomes the minimum, its lack becomes a serious impediment to future job seekers. And, clearly, as more people earn college degrees, the quality of your transcript matters more and more.

- **Your transcript can be thought of as a kind of "life credit report."** It takes ten years to fully overcome the negative effects of a bankruptcy on a person's credit history. It can take years to overcome a weak college transcript. What makes a transcript weak? Obviously, a low grade point average is a detriment on a transcript. So are lots of withdrawals and lots of fluff courses. When employers and graduate school admissions officers look at a large number of transcripts and applications, they need criteria for awarding their limited jobs or scholarships. Consequently, just about everything in your application packet is important: letters of recommendation, work history, hobbies—and the courses you took and the grades you received.

- **All the effort and careful attention will pay off.** To begin with the philosophical point first, regardless of the kind of job you get, your college education should provide you with reasoning skills, interests, cultural baggage, and character traits that will help you cope with life. On the socio-economic front, Lunenfeld and Lunenfeld report in *College Basics* that Anthony Patrick Carnevale, Ph.D., of the American Society for Training and Development, compared the potential lifetime earnings of two students, one without and one with a college degree. Dr. Carnevale calculated that the college degree would be worth about $631,000 in additional income.

- **What about all those with Ph.D.s who are driving cabs and flipping burgers?** Keep in mind that jobs requiring a doctorate are relatively rare. Many people pursue a Ph.D. hoping to get one of the few jobs in their narrow speciality. Associate of Arts and Bachelor's degrees are by far in greater demand. But more important—and realistically—a college degree provides *a greater range of job opportunities, not a guaranteed job.* Landing a good job also depends on luck and such personal characteristics as a willingness to be flexible early in your job search, choice of major, and willingness to live where the good jobs in your field are. Last, some very satisfied people (with and without Ph.D.'s) drive cabs and flip burgers. Socrates (c. 470–399 B.C.) was a brick mason, Lao-tzu (c. 575 B.C.) was a low-level bureaucrat, and Baruch Spinoza (1632–1677) was a lens grinder—three examples of wise people who preferred very ordinary jobs.

A NOTE OF ENCOURAGEMENT FOR PART-TIME STUDENTS

According to a 1993 American Council on Education study of 1,800 colleges and universities, there are more part-time students than ever before. Today, more than 40% of all college students are part-timers, and analysts expect the proportion of part-time students to increase into the foreseeable future. If you are one of these students, do your very best to make college a priority. Here are some ways to do that:

- **Write out a schedule at the start of every new school term.** Remember that failure to stick to a schedule is perhaps the greatest cause of frustration and failure for college students.

- **Regularly focus your attention on the importance and value of your long-term goals.** Consult your list of reasons for going to college. Add to it. Remind yourself *why* you are juggling family life, a job, social activities, and college: You want a satisfying life for yourself and any family you may have, and you have realistically determined that a college education is necessary for that life.

- **Read and listen to inspiring stories about struggling to get ahead.** Think of relatives who have worked hard to support you. Think of people you admire who worked hard and struggled for a mighty goal.

- **Put your frustrations in perspective.** You may be extremely busy, extremely poor, and extremely stressed-out at times; *but* people have and are suffering as much or more than you and surviving, and even growing. This suggestion is not meant to trivialize your hardships but to help you endure and master them. If life has dealt you a more difficult path than others, you have all the more reason to persist with your studies and give yourself every opportunity to have a better future than you will probably have if you drop out of college.

- **Take advantage of every support system you can find.** Many colleges provide day care for students' children. See if you qualify. Most colleges have tutorial centers, reading and writing labs, access to computers, health clinics, and special, overlooked scholarships for all sorts of things: unmarried mothers, textbook money, first-generation students, members of different ethnic groups, and so on. Ask around and shop around until you find a good adviser or counselor.

- **Remember that a six-year degree is still a degree—and a degree is what you're after.** If it takes you longer to graduate than it takes full-time students, so be it. No matter how angry or frustrated this may make you, don't let it stop you. The Stoic writer Seneca (c. 4 B.C.–65 A.D.) said, "The greater the torment, the greater shall the glory be." If you persist, you will not only have a college degree or certificate, but you will have become a stronger, wiser, more appreciative human being in the process. That's quite a payoff.

SELF-HELP

- **HALT!** That's not an order, it's an acronym—an easily remembered abbreviation for the formula: "Don't let yourself get too **H**ungry, too **A**ngry, too **L**onely, or too **T**ired." The Classical Greeks and Romans believed in a sound mind in a sound body, and contemporary science suggests that they were right. We learn best when our basic physical, emotional, and mental needs are all met.

- **Take the "walking cure."** The poet David Grayson said "There is a poem in stretched legs," and today we know that even relatively mild exercise reduces anxiety and increases our sense of well-being and happiness. Some psychologists even treat mild depression with exercise and attribute some anxieties to an overactive mind in an underactive body.

- **When in doubt, talk it out.** Sometimes the simple act of discussing problems generates solutions. Even if it doesn't, it almost always provides mental and emotional relief and restores balance and perspective.

- **Meet your obligations to yourself as well as to your family, friends, and employer in a balanced way.** You are entitled to a good education, and do not need to feel guilty for taking time for yourself to get one. You also have other responsibilities. If you fail to meet them adequately, you may find yourself distracted by guilt. If you fail to give yourself enough time to learn, you may find yourself drained by anger and resentment. Balance can be difficult to find, but it pays off.

- **Be flexible in all but the essentials.** Stick to your guns on important matters, but cut yourself slack on all others.

- **Study when you can and regularly, not just before major tests.** Not only will this improve your grades, skills, and comprehension, it will reinforce the message that learning is an integral part of your life, not something you do only under pressure. It also reduces unhealthy anxiety—a real killer.

- **Make a supreme effort to have read every assignment at least once *before* class.** You may not be able to study every page of all your assignments before every class, but you can quickly read ahead of your professors for every class. Naturally, the more time you can devote to preclass reading, the better, but even a quick reading of assigned material will pay off. You will be familiar with the purpose of each lecture or discussion. You will be more comfortable asking questions if you are familiar with the material (and hence more willing to ask questions). You will feel less anxious when you are prepared, and will remember and understand better than if you were tense or uninformed.

- **Study on schedule.** Do not wait to study until weekends and immediately before tests and assignments are due. Even if your grades don't suffer when you fall into the clutches of procrastination and "last-minute-itis," you will have robbed yourself of processing information for long-term retention and mastery. You will add anxiety to your already busy life. You will deprive yourself of full participation in class, since you won't be familiar with the material as it is covered. (Reminder: academic counselors report that failure to establish and stick to a regular study schedule is the most common characteristic shared by students who receive poor grades or who ultimately drop out of college.)

- **Get everything you're paying for.** Have you ever been glad to discover that a class has been cancelled or let out early? College is the only commodity I know of where people are happy when they don't get everything they're paying for. Sure, a change of pace is great once in a while. It can be invigorating. You can't help it when classes are cancelled, but you can resist the defeatist attitude of "Ugh! I have to go to class." Don't drag yourself to class. Attend eagerly, grateful for the opportunity to learn something new in a pleasant environment.

- **Contribute to your course by being pleasant and well prepared.** Students are sometimes surprised when they discover how much their own attitudes affect their teachers. Just as it can be very difficult to learn from unprepared, hostile, low-energy, or bored teachers, it can be very difficult to teach a class when even a few students exhibit some of these traits. On the other hand, the presence of one or two eager, well-prepared, and pleasant students always enhances the quality of a course.

- **Take classes from the best instructors you can.** Don't take classes just because they're easy. That's a form of stealing your own time. Avoiding challenges diminishes your abilities and self-esteem. (The best way to find good instructors is to ask around. Ask everybody you meet to recommend instructors. You'll quickly recognize the names of the best.)

- **Take at least one class you're afraid of—and stick it out.** Simply completing a challenging class will boost your sense of self. It will show you that you have drive and discipline. And you might discover new interests and abilities. Remember, *you* can do difficult things!

- **Take at least one class for the sheer joy of it.** Break free of the trap of the drudge, the student whose whole education is serious and calculating, allowing no room for failures (often defined as anything less than an A). A shriveled life is a pretty high price to pay for a 4.0 GPA. If you view college as something to "get over with," you will rob yourself of the *personal enrichment* that should be part of any real education. There is nothing wrong with the practical, job-preparation part of contemporary higher education. But so much more is possible, if you want it.

- **Drop classes only when absolutely necessary.** A high GPA accompanied by a high percentage of dropped courses is a red flag to university and graduate program admission committees. Do well the first time.

- **Feel free to pick your own major: Remember, it's your life.** The late mythologist Joseph Campbell used to say, "There's no greater tragedy than to get to the top of the ladder and realize you're on the wrong wall."

- **When you feel as if you'll never get done, think of this Buddhist proverb: "The journey is the destination."** There is no rule against enjoying philosophy and college.

AVOID THE BIGGEST MISTAKES COLLEGE STUDENTS MAKE

Here's a helpful list of common mistakes college students make.

- **Not making college a priority.** This can be difficult if you are a part-time student or have family obligations or work long hours at a job. But not making college a priority is one of the worst things you can do to your chances for a good education.

- **Making poor course selections.** Consult experienced students, and select courses by professors, not just course names.

- **Signing up for too many or too few classes.** Freshmen should be especially careful not to overload their schedules the first term. At the same time, taking too few classes can lead to dropping out of college if progress toward a degree takes too long. Ironically, taking too few classes can be worse than having a full schedule, if your light load gives you a false sense of security that makes sticking to a study schedule difficult. Also, taking too few credit courses can result in loss of financial aid.

- **Having poor study habits.** Poor study habits include not studying enough, studying when distracted or tired, studying in bed, and studying under the influence of drugs.

- **Being too social.** You may be likely to drop out of college if you are lonely or stressed-out because you have deleted all fun from your life; but you are just as likely to drop out if you are so busy socializing and having "the college experience" that you lose sight of the fact that getting a good education is the most important part of that experience.

- **Retaining freshman ego.** The "freshman ego" is an inflated sense of superiority that some college students retain long after they stop being freshman. This mind-set occurs when the natural joy and delight of being new to higher education, of having optimistic, idealistic goals, and of *sometimes* seeing through hypocrisy and pernicious compromise are misinterpreted as signs of profound insight and wisdom. The freshman ego is ready to fix the world. Often, its concerns are real and important: the environment, social justice, poverty, and so forth. But dogmatism (unquestioning faith in the correctness and superiority of our own ideas) is not just a hindrance to learning; it often alienates others, making it more difficult for us to communicate our ideas to them.

BE COOL ABOUT BEING COOL ABOUT SCHOOL

A word of caution: What follows is being written by a middle-aged philosophy professor who is never quite sure what the current "cool" term is. Over the course of my educational career (which began when I was 6 years old and continues to the present), the cool terms have included: *hip, hep, groovy, way out, boss, bitchin', bad, rad, radical, neat (!), fine, excellent, beautiful, copacetic, smooth, mellow*—and *cool*. But there is a kind of "cool" attitude that reflects aloofness, disdain, and detachment that has always been around, and it can really interfere with your enjoyment and success in school. That's what this section is about, whatever the current term is.

- **Sometimes, being "cool" can work against succeeding in college.** Being cool sometimes manifests itself as adopting a style that is deliberately unresponsive, aloof, antiestablishment, and distant—detached and in control of every gesture, word, and emotion. That kind of cool sits in the back of the classroom, slouches, and smirks. Cool sleeps in class. Cool wears shades. Unresponsive cool doesn't take notes. Aloof cool doesn't lug around a backpack full of textbooks. Distant cool cuts class. Antiestablishment cool shows up hung over or loaded, whispers and passes notes in class—makes its disdain very clear. Such an attitude can easily lead to a profound sense of detachment from class. It interferes with listening and learning. This kind of cool may attract unfavorable attention from the professor and from more serious, "uncool," students, which will simply reinforce an "us against them" sense of detachment.

- **Aloof cool's tendency to "dis" character traits that lead to academic and socio-economic success is a serious stumbling block to learning.** By "disrespecting"—that is, by mocking and ridiculing—students who worry about their grades and who fully participate in class, aloof cool runs the risk of shutting itself off from succeeding at anything besides being cool.

Although there are no guaranteed paths to personal, social, and economic well-being, many of the traits that make a successful, satisfied student pay off beyond college. These traits include a reasonable work ethic, fundamental reliability, personal responsibility, wide-ranging curiosity, willingness to consider new points of view, and respect for others. A strong sense of contempt for others is not conducive to good work or school relationships. Antiestablishment effort devoted to "beating the system" (through cheating on tests, scamming financial aid, purchasing term papers, conning professors) robs the cool of the sorts of experiences that foster lasting self-respect. "Beating the system" reinforces a false sense of superiority. This feeling of superiority is false because it does not take great ability to cheat teachers who have large classloads or more significant tasks than catching every attempt to get away with something. Furthermore, there's always the risk that by adopting the view that education is just one more cynical game, the distantly cool student creates a mindset that projects shabby cynicism to other aspects of life.

- **Cool cool's range of influence is surprisingly limited.** Cool cool is most appealing to people who have a heightened need for validation from other people. Cool cool is not very influential in graduate school, at most jobs, when applying for a loan, in court, and so on. It's one thing to be selectively cool, but being cool can be self-limiting if it becomes a major goal in your life.

- **Affirmative cool is wise cool.** Affirmative, or "hot," passionate cool is an attitude of delight, respect, and attraction. This is cool as a term of high praise. College is cool in this way. Studying is cool in this way of being cool. Participating in class, showing enthusiasm, being involved are cool. If you like being cool, be cool enough to maximize your time in college. Even if the sheer joys of learning and mastery don't move you, the opportunity to live a richer life, a life of more choices and opportunities, can be a sufficient motive to be a good student. And that's really cool.

CHAPTER 7

Relating To Your Professor

Your philosophy professor wants you to succeed in acquiring new knowledge, learning and polishing new skills, discovering new facets of yourself, and experiencing firsthand the many pleasures of the mind. Just as it is to your advantage to have a competent, friendly, courteous, professional instructor, it is to your instructor's advantage to have eager, inquisitive, hard-working, and courteous students. It's helpful to keep that in mind when you interact with your professor.

The following is a collection of tips and guidelines for making the most of your interactions with your professor.

- **Always respect your teacher's role and position, regardless of your feelings about the person.** If you have the unfortunate experience of being stuck with a teacher you find difficult or ineffective, remind yourself that in spite of his or her weaknesses, this teacher has successfully completed several years of higher education. At the very least, he or she is entitled to the respect due the role of teacher.

- **When you just cannot get along with your teacher, take appropriate, informed action on your own behalf.** If your teacher degrades you or others, engages in sexual harassment, or expresses bigotry or prejudice to a degree that inhibits learning, you will need to take appropriate action. You should consult with a trusted counselor or other knowledgeable individual in such a serious case. Your remedies will range from talking things over with the teacher to going to the department head or a higher-level administrator in very serious situations. If the problem is a personality or teaching style clash, you may have to choose between evils: sticking it out and doing your best, or dropping the class and taking it later from a different instructor.

- **Communicate, communicate, communicate.** Your professor cannot read your mind. It is *your responsibility* to let him or her know when something is not clear or whenever you have a special concern. Since you are responsible for all assignments, it is important to understand exactly what is expected.

- **Study the course syllabus as soon as you receive it.** Learn what is important to your instructor. Learn the location of his or her office, the designated office hours, and the office phone number.

- **Address your instructor the way he or she prefers.** Some instructors prefer to be addressed as Mr., Mrs., or Ms., others as Doctor or Professor. Simple courtesy and pragmatism suggest that you do as requested. Although some instructors prefer to be addressed by their first names, do not use an instructor's first name until invited to do so.

- **Request, don't demand.** The Taoists teach (correctly, I think) that "Forceful actions rebound." That means that aggression breeds aggression, attack breeds counterattack. No matter how nervous, frightened, or angry you are, try not to approach your instructor in a rude, belligerent, demanding, or sarcastic manner. Doing so may pollute the interaction before it begins. Instructors can be just as insecure as you are. When attacked, some of them immediately become defensive and resistant to your message.

- **Speak for yourself.** Unless seriously injured or incarcerated, do not ask parents, friends, coaches, or other instructors to speak to your instructor for you.

- **Stay in touch.** If you have to miss a few classes or cannot meet an assignment deadline or make a test date, contact your instructor as soon as you know you will not be there. Do not rely on others to convey your message. Do not just assume that you will or won't be allowed an extension. It's your responsibility to meet all requirements or make your own arrangements for not doing so.

- **Think about how you say things.** Most instructors do not appreciate remarks such as: "I missed class Tuesday. Did we do anything important?" or "That's dumb. Why'd we waste class time on it?" Consider these more effective alternatives: "I'm sorry I was not in class Tuesday. What can I study to help make up for what I missed?" "I'm not clear as to the significance of this material. Could you explain it further for me?" If you hate philosophy, there's no particular reason to volunteer that fact to the person who's devoted a lifetime to it.

- **Don't flirt with or date your instructor. Period.** Even if you think your involvement has no bearing on your grades, other students won't believe that. They'll feel cheated, and they will find out about your involvement. If you break up, you may find yourself in the awkward position of being graded by your "ex."

- **Don't tolerate sexual harassment.** If your instructor flirts with you, makes inappropriate personal comments, or somehow makes you uncomfortable in a sexual way, you are in a delicate spot. Tell your instructor you are not comfortable. If that does not take care of the problem, talk to the instructor's immediate supervisor.

- **Let your instructor know what works and what doesn't.** Instructors get less useful feedback about their courses than you might guess. Vague compliments or criticisms ("Great class!" or "Boy, was that boring!") don't help us develop and retain good features and modify or delete, bad ones. Be specific when commenting on what does or doesn't work.

- **Share your enthusiasm.** Perhaps nothing delights a teacher more than expressions of interest in a course. Ask for additional works by a favorite philosopher. Stop by and tell your instructor about a connection you've made between something from philosophy class and another class or about something that has some special relevance to your daily life.

- **Avoid appeals to pity.** If you have a special request, make it in as straightforward a way as possible. Avoid committing the logical fallacy known as *appeal to pity*. An appeal to pity occurs when a person attempts to advance a conclusion by evoking feelings of pity in others when pity is irrelevant to the conclusion at hand. If you have special circumstances that interfere with getting an assignment in on time or taking a test, you should certainly inform your instructor in a timely way. If you anticipate a persistent pattern of such requests, you may need to take the course at some other time. Appealing to pity is unwise because you never know if it will move your professor to help you or be perceived as excuse making, avoidance, or manipulation.

CONFERENCES WITH YOUR PROFESSOR

- **Always introduce yourself.** Until you're sure that your instructor knows your name, always introduce yourself and identify the particular course section you attend.

- **Make a good-faith effort to meet during scheduled office hours.** You don't want to waste your instructor's time or give the impression that you are irresponsible, so don't be irresponsible. Keep track of appointments, and if you miss one, notify your instructor as soon as possible. Whatever your reason for missing the appointment—even if it's just that you forgot—don't simply avoid mentioning it. If you don't have a good excuse, simply apologize; if you have an excuse, use it. The worst thing to do when you have any kind of problem with a class is nothing. Your philosophy instructor wants to help you succeed. He or she will work with you if you make a solid effort—and if you communicate.

- **Keep your appointments, or notify the instructor or the philosophy department secretary if you cannot.** This simple courtesy is also pragmatic: It keeps you on good terms with your professor.

- **Be on time.** Politely, let your instructor know you have arrived.

- **Knock before opening a closed office door.** If your professor's office door is closed, don't just open it.

- **After studying carefully, if there is still something you don't understand or have a problem with, write it out clearly and specifically before going to your professor.** Often, the very act of formulating a clear question or statement regarding a problem will make the answer clear to you or will point you to the answer. When this does not work, your statement will still be a great help to your professor, making it easier for him or her to help you.

- **If you have a number of questions, bring a written list of the main points you wish to discuss.** It's easy to forget even the most important things during a discussion. If you have a written list, you can make sure that you've covered everything that's important to you.

- **If you're discussing a grade, bring the test or paper with you.** Don't expect your instructor to remember the details of every test or paper.

- **Cool off before you discuss something that's really bothering you.** Don't rush right over and complain about a test or paper grade on the basis of your first reaction. Wait at least one day. Carefully reassess the issue. If it remains important to you, consult your instructor.

LETTERS OF RECOMMENDATION (AND BEYOND)

As I learned during my sophomore year in college (see "Preface"), it is difficult for most instructors to write a persuasive letter of recommendation based only on a student's grades. The most effective letters of recommendation refer to your unique qualities. Get to know three or four instructors well enough for them to recommend you personally.

As the term implies, a *letter of recommendation* is a written evaluation attesting to your abilities and recommending that you be viewed favorably as a candidate for scholarships, financial aid, admissions to academic and vocational programs, or a job. Letters of recommendation may be sent directly to those requesting them, or they may be held by your college's placement office in a file known as a *dossier*. Your dossier will also contain your current transcript. Check to see whether your school offers this service. The great advantage of having a dossier on file is that you don't need to ask for letters over and over, and you don't have to worry about losing track of them. You just place an order to have your dossier sent to whoever receives your job or school application, and the placement office mails out an official copy for a modest handling fee. You can usually add to your dossier as you get more letters of recommendation.

The most effective letters of recommendation are not seen by their subjects, which frees their writers to be very candid. Don't be disturbed if you don't get to see your letters. If you are afraid of getting a negative evaluation from a professor, do not ask him or or her for a letter. If you are given the choice between a letter you will be allowed to read or a "blind" letter, the blind letter may be a better bet because it will be interpreted as being more honest than a letter written with the knowledge that you will read it.

The most effective letters of recommendation are written by individuals with the training and experience to recognize superior merit or promise. They are specific and are based on sufficient relevant contact with you and your work. Keep this in mind when choosing people to write your letters of recommendation.

The time to deal with letters of recommendation is *immediately.* Even if you aren't sure you'll need any, play it safe and assume that you will. It can be difficult to write effective recommendations for students years after they've taken a course. With that in mind, here's a strategy for getting good letters of recommendation. This strategy pays off in other ways, too.

- **No matter what your current goals are, proceed with the assumption that at some point in your life you may need letters of recommendation from at least three of your undergraduate professors.**

- **Drop by and just say "hi."** Stop by and introduce yourself to your professors early in the term. You don't have to make a production of it or engage in "kissing up." Explain why you're taking the class, what you hope to gain from it, what your educational plans are, and so forth.

- **Speak up in class.** Show interest in your courses by being an active participant. Make thoughtful comments (if you're current with your studies).

- **Stop by when things are going well.** Reintroduce yourself, discuss what you've learned, what progress you've made, and so forth.

- **Perform at a level worthy of an honest recommendation.** Colleges, graduate programs, and potential employers look at more than just grades. Your "performance" includes: responsibility (Did you meet deadlines? Did you attend class regularly?); reliability (Did you follow instructions? Did you pay attention to details? Did you proofread your papers?); teachability (Did you give new ideas a fair hearing?); maturity (Did you take criticism well and refrain from blaming others for your problems?); citizenship (Were you respectful of others? Did you do your part to make it a good class?); self-motivation (Did you sustain a high level of effort without having to be pushed constantly?); creativity (Did you think for yourself and add your own personal style to your coursework?).

- **Don't be afraid to request a recommendation just because you didn't get an A or B in a course.** Assess your overall performance in light of all relevant factors, not just grades.

- **Demonstrate good character and motivation.** Show up for all classes, and be on time for class. Turn in assignments on time and in the proper format.

- **Show that you learn from criticism.** If weaknesses are identified in essays or papers, make sure not to repeat them in subsequent work.

- **Take more than one class from the same professor.** It is much easier for instructors to write recommendations for students they know something about. If you do well, taking additional courses from the same instructor increases the chances that the instructor will be able to write a strong letter on your behalf. Some instructors will feel uncomfortable writing a letter of recommendation for a student who has only taken one class with them, no matter how well the student did in that one class. The exception is classes that involve regular discussion, lots of writing, and office visits. In those circumstances, most instructors will be able to write effective letters of recommendation for good students.

- **Request your letter in a timely fashion.** Ask for your letter at least two weeks before you need it.

- **Politely check on your letter's progress in one week.**

- **Provide *pertinent written information* when you make your request.** It's a very good idea to provide a written statement of your plans and goals at the time you ask for a letter of recommendation. Also mention any helpful personal information: Are you a parent? Do you work? Where? How many hours? What's your major? What's your immediate goal (scholarship, 4-year transfer, graduate school, and so on)? What's your long-term goal (psychologist, philosopher, preacher, engineer, nurse, forest ranger)?

- **Provide a copy of your transcript and a list of your current courses.** Be sure to flag any courses you've taken from the instructor you're asking to write the letter.

- **Choose your letter writers wisely.** Select instructors who know your abilities and can honestly recommend you with enthusiasm. In today's world of inflated recommendations, a mediocre letter can be worse than no letter.

- **Always ask whether the instructor can comfortably write a strong letter for you.** Today's letters of recommendation are often grossly inflated. As embarrassing and disappointing as it can be to learn that your instructor doesn't feel that she can write you a strong recommendation, it's much better to learn that before a weak letter has done its damage.

- **Be sure to get some letters from instructors in courses that are relevant to your future plans.** A letter from your philosophy instructor is not likely to carry as much weight for admissions to a music program as one from your music theory instructor. Failure to provide relevant letters may arouse concern by those reviewing your application.

- **Set up a dossier file at your school's placement office.** If your school has a placement office that will keep a set of transcripts and letters for you, use it. For many years, you will be able to request that your dossier be sent to schools and prospective employers. You will not have to run around photocopying letters—if you can even find them a few years later.

- **If your instructors give you copies of their letters, keep them together in a file—and keep a backup file in a separate safe place.** This is good advice even if you are registered with the school's placement service.

- **Don't leave college without at least three letters of recommendation.** Just because you don't plan to go on in school doesn't mean you won't need letters of recommendation. People change their minds. Furthermore, good college recommendations can be used when applying for jobs, admission to police or firefighting academies, and special military programs. Potential employers will look for signs of responsibility, ambition, maturity, ability to solve problems and complete a program, and so forth.

CHAPTER 8

Test Taking

Although it may not always seem true, tests are designed to see what you have learned in a particular course, not what you don't know. Fortunately, there are basic guidelines for maximizing your chances of doing well on any kind of test. This section covers basic test preparation and specific tips for essay, short-answer, and objective tests.

PREPARING FOR TESTS

- **STUDY, STUDY, STUDY.** The single best preparation for any kind of test is practicing effective study habits on a routine basis.

- **Take advantage of "free" tests and quizzes.** If your instructor offers extra-credit tests, or drops one or more tests, make sure to take every test. Dropped or extra-credit tests amount to free practice.

- **Be sure to attend any test reviews.** Some instructors devote the class period preceding a test to last-minute questions and review. Be sure to take advantage of such an opportunity by coming to class with written questions.

- **Study as if all tests are essay tests, whether they are or not.**
  Studies have shown that students perform worse when they gear their studying to objective tests. In one experiment, one group of students was told to prepare for an essay test but was actually given an objective test. Another group of students was told to prepare for and was actually given an objective test. The students who had been expecting an essay test did markedly better. This pattern has been confirmed in other experiments.* See the subsequent section on essay tests for specific advice on studying for essay tests.

- **Avoid cramming.** Although some students insist that they learn best under pressure, research suggests caution. Too much anxiety interferes with critical thinking skills and other cognitive abilities. Memory retention markedly declines, the ability to reason diminishes, even perceptual skill decreases under extreme anxiety and stress. Also, skills classes require regular practice. Courses such as logic, critical thinking, most science, and all math courses cover both information and skills, so cramming cannot compensate for regular, incremental studying.

- **Get your normal amount of sleep the night before the test.**
  Fatigue produces and exacerbates some of the same conditions as anxiety: impaired retention of information, "processing errors" (misreading, spelling mistakes, filling in the wrong part of the exam, overlooking key instructions), and diminished thinking skills. Sleep deprivation can also trigger depression and other "down" emotions that interfere with testing well.

- **Study under conditions similar to actual testing conditions.**
  For example, avoid drinking caffeinated drinks while you study unless you are sure you can drink them during or right before the exam. Studies show that students have a much higher rate of retrieving information when their biochemical state is the same as when they learned it: Students who sipped coffee while studying did better on tests when they were allowed to sip coffee during the test than when they weren't.

---

*   Harari, H., and McDavid, J. W., "Cultural influences on retention of logical and symbolic material." *Journal of Educational Psychology*, 57, 1966, p. 18; Harkness, D. R., "A surgical approach to large classes." *Journal of Educational Psychology*, 17, 1965, p. 179; Myer, G., "The effect of examination set on memory." *Journal of Educational Psychology*, 25, 1934, p. 641.

- **Eat wisely before the test.** Don't eat a big meal or candy bar right before the test. The last thing you want to experience during a test is that drowsy feeling that can follow a big meal. But do eat and drink lightly before the test. When your blood sugar is too low during a test, you can feel shaky, weak, and confused. You will also be confused if you're severely dehydrated.

- **Allow extra time to get to class on test day.** Again, do all that you can to avoid disruptive anxiety. Get to class early enough to select your usual seat; make sure you have any necessary pens, pencils, paper, bluebooks, notes (if allowed).

- **VERY IMPORTANT TIP: Always pick up your graded test and attend class the day the test is discussed.** Your grade is not the only thing that matters. Learning from mistakes and correcting errors will pay off on subsequent tests. Collecting and studying each and every test is the first step in preparing for your next test.

RELAXATION TECHNIQUES FOR BETTER TEST SCORES

Practice the following relaxation techniques—especially if you tend to panic on tests:

- **Stretch slowly and leisurely before taking your seat.**

- **Remind yourself that your performance on the test, no matter how important, does not measure your worth as a human being or predict your chances of finding ultimate happiness.**

- **Remind yourself that you are already a test-taking expert.** You've already taken hundreds, if not thousands, of tests in grade school and high school, perhaps in the military or applying for a job.

- **Take a tip from successful athletes and performers:** *Visualize yourself taking the test and doing well.* *Creative visualization* is not the same thing as vaguely imagining something. Visualization is not a dreamy fantasy but a detailed, focused, highly concentrated, carefully structured, step-by-step mental imaging of a future event—in this case, the test. Sports and performance psychologists report that creative visualization can enhance the effectiveness of *prepared and capable* athletes and performers in a variety of fields. Visualization is not a substitute for solid preparation.

- **Practice deep breathing.** Force yourself to breathe deeply and slowly, especially when you are nervous and your natural inclination is to hyperventilate.

- **Immediately after you receive the test, put the test face down, close your eyes, place both hands on the desk, and breathe slowly and deeply for a few seconds.** Tell yourself that you will do well. These few seconds can save you from rushing into the test in a state of unproductive anxiety. By taking conscious control of your bodily movements, you can inhibit the panicky sense that often accompanies rapid breathing and a quick pulse.

- *Slowly* **turn your test over,** *slowly* **read it through,** *slowly* **pick up your pencil, and then go to work.** Consciously avoid the kind of jerky, "hyper" movements associated with panic or fear. Such movements actually reinforce and stimulate panic or fear. Monitor your breathing, too. When you feel panicked, put your pencil down and practice deep breathing for a few seconds.

- **Be thankful for a *touch of anxiety.*** A bit of anxiety can be an advantage because moderately heightened adrenal function (short of a panic level) *increases cognitive and perceptual acuity.* Some test anxiety is normal and usually helpful.

HOW TO DO YOUR BEST ON ESSAY TESTS

- *Read* **the whole test** *before answering any questions.*

- **Follow all instructions.** Note the time limit, if any. Note whether you must answer all questions or only some. Pay attention to the relative value of questions.

- **Familiarize yourself with *all* questions before answering *any.*** This will allow you to organize a strategy for getting the most correct answers. Furthermore, the answer to one question may remind you of the answer to another.

- **First answer the questions you know the most about.** Don't worry if these questions aren't worth as much as other questions. Beginning from strength has a number of advantages: You can get right to work, thus maximizing your time. You're sure to have some correct answers. You'll boost your confidence and reduce anxiety. You'll kick your mind into gear quickly, and avoid the panic and confusion that can result from wrestling with a question that draws a blank.

- **When in doubt, write.** If you can't think of anything to write about any question, write something about one of them anyway. On scratch paper preferably (if scratch paper is allowed), write down anything you can remember that's even remotely connected to the question. If you keep writing, you'll probably discover information, connections, and patterns that seemed beyond reach. You may have to scrap most of this "creative" writing once your mind kicks into gear, and write a more polished essay, but that's all right.

- **Be neat.** Your instructor should not have to decipher bad handwriting or decode crossed-out passages or convoluted arrows connecting a sentence on page 2 to one on page 4. If you must make extensive corrections to an essay answer, completely and clearly cross out the undesired work. Ask the instructor or proctor if you can begin on a new sheet of paper, if necessary.

- **If you are responsible for providing your own bluebooks or paper, be sure to have plenty of the kind specified.** Some instructors require their students to bring in bluebooks a class period or two before the test. They then check to ensure that the bluebooks are blank, and may stamp or sign them to indicate this. Allow ample time to buy your bluebooks and take extra precautions not to fold or wrinkle them. Your instructor may refuse to grade a test written on unapproved paper or in an unapproved bluebook.

- **Don't substitute your own paper without asking, and don't go fishing around through your notebook or book bag for paper or pens, or anything else.** You might know you're not cheating, but your instructor may not.

- **Use complete sentences; don't use obscure abbreviations; use good grammar.** Essay tests ask for *essays*, not collections of fragmentary notes. Bad grammar is almost always associated with cloudy thinking. At the very least, bad grammar weakens your ideas.

- **Spell all technical terms and proper names correctly.** There is absolutely no excuse for not learning how to spell the important terms that are introduced as part of a course. This applies to terms derived from Greek, Latin, and other languages that are difficult for you. The fact that a word is unusual or hard to pronounce just means that you have to work a little harder to become comfortable with it.

- **Mention specific relevant examples, persons, titles, and so forth from assigned readings, the textbook, and the instructor's lectures.** Be specific. Show that you are knowledgeable in terms of *this class*. Essay tests have two functions: to show that you can think on a sophisticated level *and* to show that you have acquired new information. Your essays should always present information in a coherent fashion.

- **Make and *show* connections; don't just list facts and information.** Avoid the extremes of both the overly general essay that does not reveal an adequate fund of information, and the "pseudo-essay" that is so crammed with facts that it is not a coherent essay at all.

- **Make sure you answer the question that is asked.** Pay attention to such instructions as "compare and contrast," "explain why," "analyze," and so forth. Follow instructions. Your instructor may not give credit for wonderful insights, no matter how brilliantly expressed, if they are not responsive to the question *as it is framed*.

- **Don't combine questions.** Even if the answers to two or three questions overlap, it's best to answer each question separately and exactly as it asked. Grading essays is hard work, and most instructors will find evaluating combined essays especially difficult, because even related questions call for different emphasis and analysis.

- **Keep track of the time.** Don't try to write perfect essays. You might spend too much time on one or two questions. Allow time for a quick scan of all your answers at the end of the period so you can catch any glaring errors or omissions.

- **Answer every required question.** Partial credit (no matter how little) is far better than no credit. Your instructor has good reasons for the combination of questions included on your test, so don't defeat them by avoiding the required questions. Every once in a while I have a student answer extra optional questions to "compensate" for not answering one or more required questions. This never works. It's like having a mechanic adjust your brakes when you have a steering problem—because he's not able to fix the steering.

- **Reread your answer before turning it in.** Consider proofreading your answer as a vital part of writing it. It may be tempting (and common) to write up to the last second, but it is more effective not to have to. This is another reason to be very well prepared for the test: you will be able to start writing right away, and will have lots of valuable things to say.

- **Write a clear conclusion/summation that uses key phrases and examples from your essay (just as you would for an out-of-class assignment).** Psychologically, a lucid, focused conclusion encourages your reader to look more favorably on your essay instead of stopping in the middle of

HOW TO DO YOUR BEST ON COMPLETION TESTS

- **Read the entire test before answering any questions.** Later questions may contain useful information for answering earlier questions, and vice-versa. Reading the entire test gives you the "lay of the land," so you can maximize your time by first going quickly through questions you know very well and then concentrating on more complex or difficult questions.

- **Follow instructions.** This is always important, but it is crucial when tests are scored by teaching assistants or student aides who may not have the expertise or authority to deal with improvisations or modifications of the requested format.

- **Use the kind of pen or pencil required, and be very careful when you fill in your answers or erase them.** It is difficult and tiring to read light, brightly colored inks and very light (hard) pencil lead. You should always use black or blue ink or a No. 2 pencil, unless your instructor specifies otherwise.

- **Spell technical terms and proper names correctly.** Do not abbreviate. *Always* assume that spelling counts.

- **Write legibly.**

- **Confine your answers to the space allowed.** If you are allowed to use additional space, mark your continuations very clearly. But always ask before assuming you can use additional space.

- **Answer every question.** In most cases, you will be graded on the number of correct answers (check to be sure). An empty blank and a wrong answer are both worth zero. You have nothing to lose by writing something (and you may be correct and not know it). You might get partial credit.

- **Don't waste time dwelling on difficult questions.** Keep going, and come back to difficult questions after you've made one complete pass through the test.

- **Review the test before you turn it in.** The review process does more than catch omissions and errors, it can also trigger answers that were just out of reach before.

HOW TO DO YOUR BEST ON OBJECTIVE TESTS

- **Read the entire test before answering any questions.** Later questions may contain useful information for answering earlier questions, and vice-versa. Reading the entire test gives you the "lay of the land," so you can maximize your time by first going quickly through questions you know very well, and then concentrating on more complex or difficult questions.

- **Follow instructions.** This is always important, but it is crucial when tests are machine scored.

- **If your test will be machine scored, use the kind of pen or pencil required, and be very careful when you fill in your answers or erase them.** The most common grading machines are made to read clearly defined, heavy black pencil markings. The safest kind of pencil to use is the No. 2 type. No. 2 grade lead is soft enough to make a dark mark, but hard enough not to smudge. Some machines require special pencils.

- **If you are responsible for providing your own machine-scored answer sheets, be sure to bring two or three forms of the kind specified.** Allow ample time to buy your answer sheets, and take extra precautions not to fold or wrinkle them. Your instructor may refuse to grade an answer sheet that cannot be read by the grading machine.

- **Answer the easiest questions first.** You want to score as many correct answers as quickly as possible. Also, the positive experience of providing correct answers will boost your confidence, minimize test anxiety, and probably help you recall the answers to at least some of the questions that you passed over before.

- **If all questions are of equal weight, don't dawdle over difficult questions until you have made one complete pass through the test.**

- **Pay attention to key words and phrases; underline them *if you're allowed to*.** Key words include qualifiers like: *always, never, usually, mostly, sometimes, not, in part, without exception.* Watch for important qualifiers like: *according to the text,* or *in lecture.*

- **On true-false questions, pay special attention to universal terms like *always, all,* and *never*.** Such terms allow for no exceptions. If you're not sure of the answer to a question containing universal qualifiers, your best guess is false.

- **On multiple-choice questions, mentally turn each choice into a true-false question.** The leading statement plus the correct choice always yields a true statement (assuming only one correct answer). After you've chosen an answer, read the leading statement plus your choice to see if they produce a true statement. Here's a simple example:

10. Plato was the pupil of _____ and the teacher of _____.

   A. Aristotle, Socrates
   B. Diogenes, Socrates
   C. Socrates, Aristotle
   D. Aristotle, Alexander the Great
   E. None of these

The correct answer is C. If we add C to the leading statement, we get: "Plato was the pupil of *Socrates* and the teacher of *Aristotle.*" This is a true statement. No other choice produces a true statement when added to the leading statement.

- **On multiple-choice questions, always choose the most precise correct answer if more than one choice is correct.** If you are expected to select the best option on multiple-choice questions, it helps to think of selecting one option as *rejecting the other options*. Here's an example from a logic test to help illustrate this point. In this class, an argument was defined as *a group of propositions, one of which (the conclusion), is claimed to follow logically from other propositions (premises).* Which answer would you select as the "best" answer based on the italicized definition?

28. An argument consists of _____.

   A. a group of propositions
   B. at least one premise
   C. a conclusion
   D. A, B, and C
   E. None of these

Congratulations if you picked D; it's the best answer. A, B, and C are each correct in the sense that an argument does contain a group of propositions (A), one of which is the conclusion (C), and at least one of which is a premise (B). The problem with picking A, B, or C is a function of the nature of multiple-choice questions: *picking the one best multiple-choice option has the effect of denying all of the other options.* This can be illustrated easily by analyzing exactly what's involved with picking option A. Picking option A amounts to saying this: "An argument consists of <u>a group of propositions</u>, but *not* at least one premise and *not* a conclusion." Picking B amounts to saying: "An argument consists of <u>at least one premise</u>, but *not* a group of propositions and *not* a conclusion." Picking C amounts to saying: "An argument consists of <u>a conclusion</u>, but *not* a group of propositions and *not* at least one premise." Picking E is the worst possible answer.

- **Do not look for patterns among the answers; answer each question independently.** Don't worry about how many "true's" or how many "C's" there are. It is quite possible that by accident or diabolical instructor scheming all the answers are true or C—or no answer is C or true, and so forth.

- **Answer each question exactly as it is worded; don't "mentally correct" or rewrite it.** It is unfortunately quite common for students to mentally ignore key words or phrases in questions, or to "correct" them.

  Here's an example of mentally correcting a question: I once assigned random ID numbers to students to use in posting grades. The first-day syllabus stated, "You must put your random ID number on all tests, once you have been assigned a number. *No assignments will be graded without this number.*" The second week of class I gave a test over the course syllabus. I had not yet assigned random numbers. One of the true-false questions was "You must put your random ID number on all tests." Every student picked true. The correct answer was false. To be true the statement would have to be amended as follows: "You must put your random ID number on all tests, *once you have been assigned a number.*"

  The class accused me of nit-picking and being unfair. I pointed out that the statement was obviously false *since no one was required to use a random number on this very test!* I explained that since this was a test for which a random number was not required, the statement "You must put your random ID number on *all* tests" had to be false. Quite a few students said something like this: "I figured you didn't mean this test. I figured you *meant* once we have our numbers ..." In other words, those students modified the wording of the question; they mentally altered it according to their own ideas of how it should read.

- **Don't mentally add or delete phrases to questions.** (See the preceding discussion). You might do this without being aware of it. Next time you're going over a corrected test, be alert for this tendency. See whether you are somehow altering the questions from their actual wording.

- **If a question seems utterly unintelligible or lacking any correct answer, ask your instructor for clarification.** The worst that can happen is that you're told that the question is correct. Then you can rethink it or go on to questions you can answer. But you might be right. Tests do contain errors.

- **Change answers only if you have good reasons.** Statistically, more students change from correct answers to incorrect ones, but not always. Don't be afraid to change an answer if you have a good reason to.

- **Double-check your answer sheet before turning it in.** Make sure you've used the proper kind of pen or pencil and erased cleanly. Count your answers and check to see if you've skipped a line or put two answers on one line.

HOW TO DO YOUR BEST ON MIXED-QUESTION TESTS

- **On tests containing more than one kind of question, answer multiple-choice first, true-false second, fill-in third, and essay last.** Read the entire test first, and budget your time according to the relative weight of each section. Don't dwell on questions that are not worth much. Answer specific, objective questions first to reinforce basic information about the material. Allow time to reread and change answers.

- **Be sure you understand the rules for matching-type questions.** Can the same choice be used to match more than one item? Must every choice be used? Be very clear on these conditions. If they are not stated on the test, ask your instructor.

- **As always, be sure to reread your answers before turning in your test.**

- **Remember: Your best bet is to study as if all tests are essay tests.**

CONCLUSION

All things excellent are as difficult as they are rare.

Baruch Spinoza

If you've learned anything from this book, I hope it's that you have a great deal of influence over your grade in philosophy, and your entire college experience. The tips and advice in *How to Get the Most Out of Philosophy, Second Edition,* can help you avoid certain pitfalls and increase your chances of success—but they cannot provide you with the will and the drive necessary to succeed.

The *wish* to do well is common. The *will* and sustained drive to do well are less common. Regardless of your past performance in school and regardless of your "native ability," you can take deliberate, time-tested steps to improve your chances of learning philosophy and getting a good grade in the process. There are no substitutes for regular, organized effort, however.

You probably won't be able (or want) to follow every suggestion in this book. That's to be expected. Try out a few ideas that seem most helpful given your current strengths and weaknesses. Wisdom advises that although we cannot do everything, we can at least do something.

Decide right now that you want a full, rich *education*, the kind of education that goes beyond merely getting a job and degree (as important as they may be). Getting a degree is not the same thing as getting an education. All around us we see college-educated experts dumping garbage into our waterways, robbing people of their pensions, or just being dissatisfied and unhappy. Sadly, *not every college graduate is well educated.*

You will discover that when your focus shifts from just getting a grade and a degree to learning many things of value, your whole attitude becomes more receptive to learning. Grades do count, but they're not all that counts.

It's easy to forget that this is *your* education. Customize it. Work at it. *You are invited to participate in "the great conversation."* Socrates guided others out of the cave of ignorance, but they provided the effort. I offer you a map to help you on your way to wisdom. The next step is yours.

Say not, "When I have leisure I will study." Perhaps you will have no leisure.—Hillel

BEGINNING PHILOSOPHER'S BIBLIOGRAPHY

Following is a list of books about writing, thinking, and succeeding in college. I have included focused, brief books that can be read quickly or studied on an as-needed basis, if you wish to supplement the material in this book.

PHILOSOPHICALLY ORIENTED STUDY BOOKS

Sylvan Barnet and Hugo Bedau, editors. *Critical Thinking, Reading, and Writing: A Brief Guide to Argument*. Boston: Bedford Books of St. Martin's Press, 1993. This 230-page book includes a good chapter on sources and documentation.

Zachary Seech. *Writing Philosophy Papers*. Belmont, Calif.: Wadsworth Publishing Company, 1993. An excellent guide to writing philosophy papers, this 134-page text is valuable not only to philosophy students; its contents can be applied to any critical writing assignments.

Mark B. Woodhouse. *A Preface to Philosophy*, Fifth Edition. Belmont, Calif.: Wadsworth Publishing Company, 1994. This 174-page survey of what philosophy is all about includes a handy glossary of philosophical terms.

PHILOSOPHY REFERENCE BOOKS

Peter A. Angeles. *Dictionary of Philosophy*. New York: Barnes & Noble Books, 1981.

Frederick Copleston, S. J. *A History of Philosophy*. New York: Doubleday, Image edition, 1985.

The Encyclopedia of Philosophy, Ed. Paul Edwards. New York: Macmillan & Free Press, 1967.

F. E. Peters. *Greek Philosophical Terms: A Historical Lexicon*. New York: New York University Press, 1967.

Ben-Ami Scharfstein. *The Philosophers: Their Lives and the Nature of Their Thought*. Oxford: Oxford University Press, 1989.

GENERAL STUDY SKILLS

James Deese and Ellin K. Deese. *How to Study*, Third Edition Revised. New York: McGraw-Hill Book Company, 1979. Don't be fooled by the copyright date. This 120-page primer concentrates on reading; a minor classic.

Ron Fry. *"Ace" any Test*. Hawthorne, N.J.: Career Press, 1992. I found this to be a zippy, witty, practical 96-page handbook.

J. J. Gibbs. *Dancing with Your Books: The Zen Way of Studying*. New York: Penguin Books, 1990. This 181-page surprise is elegant and soothing; a book worth keeping.

Marvin Lunenfeld and Peter Lunenfeld. *College Basics: How to Start Right and Finish Strong*. Buffalo, N. Y.: Semester Press, 1991. This 144-page college self-help book, written by a father and son who are also a professor and student, packs a lot of useful material into a modest size.

Virginia Voeks. *On Becoming an Educated Person: An Orientation to College and Life*. Philadelphia: Saunders College Publishing, 1979. This is an excellent, wise, and substantial (248 pages) book that really lives up to its title.

SPECIALIZED SUBJECTS

Stephen S. Carey. *A Beginner's Guide to Scientific Method*. Belmont, Calif.: Wadsworth Publishing Company, 1994. This clearly written, 124-page book helps students master the critical thinking skills that are specific to science through the use of entertaining and worthwhile exercises.

Roseann Giarrusso, Judith Richlin-Klonsky, William G. Roy, and Ellen Strenski. *A Guide to Writing Sociology Papers*, Third Edition. New York: St. Martin's Press, 1994. This 180-page study guide for sociology students includes writing samples and strategies.

Richard Manning Smith. *Mastering Mathematics: How to Be a Great Math Student*, Second Edition. Belmont, Calif.: Wadsworth Publishing Company, 1994. At 198 pages, this weighs in as one of the most effective how-to books on the market.

SIX GUIDES TO BETTER WRITING

Philosophy instructors tend to accept any consistent commonly used system of citations. The Chicago, MLA, and Turabian style guides are the most commonly used formats for most subject areas. *The Blair Handbook* is a comprehensive (910 pages) guide to the entire writing process. Psychology students may be required to use the complicated APA style for term papers and essays.

Chicago Manual of Style, 14th Edition. Chicago: University of Chicago Press, 1993.

Toby Fulwer and Alan R. Hayakawa. *The Blair Handbook*. Englewood Cliffs, N.J.: Prentice Hall, 1994.

Joseph Garibaldi and Walter S. Achert. *MLA Handbook for Writers of Research Papers*, Third Edition. New York: Modern Language Association, 1988.

Publication Manual of the American Psychological Association, Fourth Edition. Washington, D. C.: American Psychological Association, 1994.

William Strunk, Jr., and E. B. White. *Elements of Style*, Third Edition. New York: Macmillan, 1979.

Kate L. Turabian. *A Manual for Writers of Term Papers, Theses, and Dissertations*. Chicago: University of Chicago Press, 1973.